AUTHOR BRIDGES

TITLE FRANCE under RICHELIEU

# FRANCE UNDER RICHELIEU
## AND COLBERT

MACMILLAN AND CO., Limited
LONDON · BOMBAY · CALCUTTA
MELBOURNE

THE MACMILLAN COMPANY
NEW YORK · BOSTON · CHICAGO
DALLAS · SAN FRANCISCO

THE MACMILLAN CO. OF CANADA, Ltd.
TORONTO

# FRANCE

UNDER

# RICHELIEU AND COLBERT

BY THE LATE

## JOHN HENRY BRIDGES, M.B., F.R.C.P.

SOMETIME FELLOW OF ORIEL COLLEGE, OXFORD
AND MEDICAL METROPOLITAN INSPECTOR TO THE LOCAL GOVERNMENT BOARD

A NEW EDITION

WITH AN INTRODUCTION BY

## A. J. GRANT, M.A.

PROFESSOR OF HISTORY IN THE UNIVERSITY OF LEEDS
AUTHOR OF ' THE FRENCH MONARCHY : 1483-1789,' ETC.

MACMILLAN AND CO., LIMITED
ST. MARTIN'S STREET, LONDON

1912

# INTRODUCTION

BOOKS on history grow old rapidly, and few of them take a permanent place in literature. The story of the past has constantly to be rewritten in the light of fresh research, and quite as much in the light of fresh experiences and new ideas as to the development of society. The life of Lectures is even shorter than that of books. Their aim is usually to interest and to stimulate, and they depend largely for their value on the personality of the lecturer. They rarely deserve printing, and if printed they quickly disappear from notice.

Yet here are Lectures which after the lapse of nearly half a century are republished, and their republication meets a genuine need. The original volume has been long out of print, and has only been obtainable second-hand and at a high price. It is a real service to the study of history to procure access to it for a wider public.

These Lectures have lived and continued to claim attention for reasons which it is not difficult to discover. They are in the first place exceedingly well written. The language is clear ; there is no orna-

mentation ; no purple patches are introduced ; yet
the writer claims and holds the attention on every
page. But the real value of the book lies in the
thought, not in the style. It is emphatically one
of those books which challenge and provoke thought.
The thesis which Dr. Bridges maintains is not often
to be found in English historians of France, and is
nowhere to be found in so convincing a form. He
writes in full sympathy with the Revolution of 1789,
which marks in his view the greatest change in
human history, but he does not therefore regard the
old Monarchy as a tyranny, or Henry IV, Louis XIII,
and Louis XIV as enemies of the human race, and
Richelieu, Mazarin, and Colbert as the odious agents
of crowned malefactors. He sees, on the contrary,
in the Monarchy the preparation for the Revolution ;
not as Carlyle did, because the rule of the Kings of
France created the evils against which the Revolution
was a protest ; but because, in the view of Dr. Bridges,
the royal government was destroying the power though
not the privileges of the nobles, was unifying France
in customs, language, and laws, was in fact creating
the nation which assumed sovereignty to itself in the
Revolution.

The views which Dr. Bridges expresses are largely
drawn from the philosophy of Comte, to whose interpretation he devoted nearly all his literary effort.
But the book is not propagandistic in any narrow
sense or in any sense at all which would imply

censure or raise suspicion in the reader. He has
endeavoured (and with conspicuous success) to
present the history of the French monarchy as a
part of the development of Western Europe, to
bring out its connection with the past and its legacy
to the future. So that in Dr. Bridges' hands the
history of the time is very far from 'a tale full of
sound and fury, signifying nothing,' but is on the
contrary profoundly significant ; and he has not
hesitated to sit in judgment, or to allow the succeeding centuries to sit in judgment, on kings, ministers,
poets, and philosophers. Few books in history are
written in this spirit now. Historians for the most
part fear to generalize and to judge, or think it their
duty to refrain from doing so. But books written
in this colourless way, though they have their use
and their justification, cannot arrest the attention
and stimulate reflection as a book does which, like
the present one, recognises that right and wrong are
the most important of realities for the past as well as
for the present.

The Lectures are republished almost as they
appeared in the first edition of 1866. A few mis-
prints have been corrected ; a few dates altered ; one
or two notes [1] added, but that is all. Even the allusions
to contemporary events have been allowed to stand.
They are interesting in themselves, and could not
have been omitted without a good deal of alteration

---

[1] These additional notes have been placed in brackets, to distinguish
them from the author's footnotes.

in what was left. Much of the charm of the book depends upon the impression it gives of the personality of the author, and any change in the text would necessarily diminish that feature of the work.

I desire to express my gratitude to Mr. H. Gordon Jones for many valuable suggestions and corrections, and for having relieved me of the task of seeing the book through the press.

A. J. GRANT.

Leeds University.

# AUTHOR'S PREFACE

THESE Lectures were originally delivered before the Philosophical Institution of Edinburgh, under the title of the ' Age of Louis XIV.' But the title here given seemed more appropriate.

Of the six eminent rulers of France during the seventeenth century, the first two, Henry IV and Sully, do not fall within the period here treated. Of the remaining four,—Richelieu, Mazarin, Colbert, and Louis XIV,—the first and third have a better claim than the second, and certainly than the fourth, to connect their names with the Culmination of the French Monarchy and the splendid intellectual development with which it was simultaneous.

From the accession of Richelieu to the death of Colbert, we have a period of about sixty years. At Richelieu's death in 1642, Antoine Arnauld, Descartes, Corneille, Poussin, had reached their prime. Pascal, Molière, Le Sueur, Puget, had attained or were approaching manhood. At Colbert's death in 1683,

Descartes, Molière, and Pascal had long ago dis-appeared ; Corneille was in his last year. Racine and La Fontaine had written most of their best works. The last thirty years of Louis XIV's reign were not indeed so totally barren of intellect as Mr. Buckle has asserted. But the palm of genius, as Voltaire recognised so frankly, had passed for awhile from France to the country of Locke and Newton.

# CONTENTS

## LECTURE I

### FORMATION OF THE FRENCH MONARCHY

xi

# CONTENTS

## LECTURE II

### INTERNAL CONDITION OF FRANCE UNDER MAZARIN AND COLBERT

## LECTURE III

### RELATIONS OF FRANCE TO EUROPE UNDER RICHELIEU, MAZARIN, AND LOUIS XIV

# CONTENTS

## LECTURE IV

### PROGRESS OF THOUGHT DURING THE SEVENTEENTH CENTURY

# CONTENTS

# LECTURE I

## FORMATION OF THE FRENCH MONARCHY

THE views held in the present day of the value and purpose of historical study, are so various, so contradictory, and so ill defined, that it is well for a lecturer on any historical period to prepare his audience, in as few words as possible, for the general line of treatment which he intends to take.

Those who have not accustomed themselves to regard human affairs as subject to any constant laws of co-existence and succession, to whom the phenomena of society and of man seem swayed by oscillations as indefinite and arbitrary as those of the solar system seemed a few centuries ago, or those of the winds and clouds till very recently, will be interested in isolated periods of history merely as they would listen to an exciting drama. They will study the play of opposing passions, the plastic influence of strong wills and master minds ; or, if their turn be more practical, may draw vague and trite maxims from the spectacle of great crimes followed by great calamities ; may moralize on the vicissitudes of fortune and the downfall of empires ; and may flatter themselves that in studying history they are

B

listening to philosophy teaching by example. Such readers will frequent, I say, isolated fields of history where the dramatic interest is high, the play of passion fierce and hot, the character of the chief actors strongly marked, or where the narrower sympathies of the spectator are roused by appeals to patriotism or sectarian feeling. But in history as a connected whole they will take but slight interest. For the Past of the human race has never presented itself to their minds as a continuous and progressive development, subject, like all other phenomena of the universe, to invariable and ascertainable laws.

It is, however, from this latter point of view that the subject of this course of lectures has been regarded. To those who look at the history of the advanced portion of our race—at the history, that is, of Southern and Western Europe and its colonies,—as the continuous and uninterrupted growth of one vast organism, each century will be seen to form an organic part of the living whole, and, apart from that whole, to have no separate life nor meaning. For the last two centuries this conception has gradually been growing into full and fuller prominence. ' The present,' said Leibnitz, ' is the creation of the past, and is big with the future.' 'The human race,' said Pascal, in the same century, ' is a colossal man, ever growing and ever learning.' Such glimpses of a stupendous truth, developed in subsequent generations by Vico in Italy, by Kant and Herder in Germany, by Turgot and Condorcet in France, have formed the starting-point of the great intellectual achievement of our own century, the historical and social philosophy of Auguste Comte.

So much seemed necessary to premise as the keynote to what follows. For the leading question to be dealt with in these lectures, the question which more or less visibly will underlie the whole series, is, What place in the chain of universal history does the age of Louis XIV occupy? How far can we see it to be consequent on the previous history of France and of Europe? What permanent results did it bequeath to the future, to the eighteenth century, and to all future time? It is obvious that this mode of treatment, if consistently carried out, will exclude the vast mass of dramatic anecdote and amusing detail which fills two hundred volumes of contemporary memoirs, and which, always entertaining and sometimes instructive as it may be, is for the most part wholly foreign to the purpose of these lectures. Nor will military campaigns and glorious victories be alluded to other than in the most cursory manner ; their results only so far as they are permanently important being stated. I propose, in the present lecture, to sketch very rapidly the rise and progress of the French monarchy. I shall point out its importance as an intermediate stage between the Catholic feudalism from which it sprang and the republican institutions for which it prepared the way. Briefly mentioning the names and the achievements of its successive founders, I shall dwell at greater length on the last and greatest, the establisher of the national unity, the destroyer of feudalism, the predecessor of the Revolution ; Cardinal de Richelieu. The internal government of France during the reign of Louis XIV will be the subject of the second lecture. Our attention will principally be fixed on the splendid yet abortive efforts of Colbert to develop the industrial and mental resources of France, to advance peacefully towards the modern era, and to attain the results of the great Revolution without the putrescent decay and the disastrous struggle. The third lecture will deal with the relations of France to Europe, from the Peace of Westphalia to the Peace of Utrecht. Richelieu will come again before us as the first of European statesmen, the founder of that system of equilibrium of States, without which the free development of Western Europe during the last two centuries would have been impossible. We shall see how and why France under Louis XIV degenerated from Richelieu's principles, and was the first to incur the penalties which that great statesman had pre-appointed for their infraction. In my last lecture I shall endeavour to characterize that which underlies all social and political agitations, and is the key to their right interpretation, the progress of European thought during the period that we are considering.

The movement of Western Europe during the last five centuries, complex, various, confused as it seems at first sight to be, may be more clearly comprehended by distinguishing its two separate processes ; the destruction of what is effete and old, the construction of the new. Decomposition, more or less rapid, of the Catholic and feudal mode of life ; gradual accumulation of fresh materials, scientific and industrial, to supply its place : these are the two distinct aspects of modern history. The ancient mode of life, based morally on belief in the dogmas of the Church, and on subjection to the spiritual authorities by whom those dogmas were interpreted ;

based politically on the feudal institutions handed
down from the Roman Empire, and modified more
or less by the Celts and Teutons, who adopted the
imperial institutions ; the military spirit dominant,
though restrained from the offensive warfare of
ancient Rome, and limited to the defence of Christendom against Mohammedan and Pagan ; the military
caste supreme over every other ; the military life,
outside the Church, the only honourable life ; the
great mass of the working population elevated,
indeed, above their condition in ancient Rome, no
longer liable to be bought and sold, possessing the
elementary rights of the family, but bound to the
soil, and politically unrecognised,—elevated, in fact,
from slavery to serfage, but not yet from serfage to
freedom ; industry tolerated, but not yet held in
honour ; commerce neglected, or abandoned to a
degraded or persecuted race : this mediæval mode
of life, called for the sake of precision Catholic
Feudalism, under which men had lived, and in spite
of modern prejudice had lived nobly, for many
centuries, was becoming, towards the close of the
thirteenth century, intolerable to men ; and its
gradual decomposition, a process which in most
countries is very far from complete, is one of the
two chief aspects of modern history.

The other aspect is the inverse process of construction of the new system of life destined to
supersede and replace the old ; the system based on
industrial activity and scientific conviction, as opposed
to the military activity and the supernatural beliefs
of the Middle Ages. When we speak of one era, of
one series of centuries as sharply opposed to another,

we do so for the sake of clearness.   In every subject
of thought the mind requires distinctions to be
drawn far more definitely than they exist in nature.
The zoologist defines the animal and vegetable
world, or demarcates the Mollusca from the Radiata,
although in actual fact the transitions from one
order or kingdom to another are imperceptible.   So
it is with History.   In saying that modern life is
opposed to ancient and to mediæval life by the substitution of industry for warfare, it is not meant that
men in ancient days did not weave or spin, buy or
sell, or that in modern centuries they did not fight ;
what is meant is, that military thoughts and purposes
were paramount, that the military class preponderated in ancient Rome, and, to a somewhat less
degree, in the Middle Ages ; whereas in modern
times industrial thoughts and purposes have become
more and more paramount, and the industrial or
capitalist class has been, for four or five centuries,
rapidly tending to become supreme.   The mercantile
class was in ancient Rome, or even in mediæval
Paris, of secondary importance ; it is now rapidly
becoming of primary importance.   Industry, which
used to be the work of slaves or serfs, is now the
work of free men.   Warfare, which once occupied
the entire life of the free citizen, is now the special
occupation of a subordinate class.   The progress of
this marvellous substitution of industry for warfare
is then one of the master facts of modern history.
And correlatively with this prodigious revolution in
the secular world, we find a similar change in the
spiritual.   Scientific conviction in every branch of
thought, whether in astronomy, in physics, in politics,

or in morals, has taken the place, or is rapidly taking the place, of the supernatural beliefs of the ancient or mediæval world. Not that there are no students of theology now, or that there were no astronomers or mathematicians in Athens, or in mediæval Paris or Oxford ; but that scientific investigation and method, applied to every branch of thought, to the motions of the heavens or to the changes of society and the precepts of morality, has been for the last four centuries more and more completely concentrating the efforts of the master spirits of the time. The spiritual leadership which from the fifth to the thirteenth century was held by Augustine, Gregory, Hildebrand, Thomas Aquinas, and St. Bernard, men who devoted their high powers to the maintenance of the supernatural dogmas of the Church, has been possessed in later centuries by Kepler, Bacon, Galileo, Descartes, Newton, and Leibnitz.

The gradual downfall of the Catholic-Feudal system ; the gradual growth of the new industrial scientific system : such, then, are the two essential features of the history of Western Europe during the last five centuries. In each successive period the progress of this double movement is the primary object to be kept steadily in view ; and the business of the lecturer is to clear it from all the accidental and insignificant detail, by which, in most historical writing, it is encumbered and concealed. And here it must be borne in mind, as one of the fundamental truths without which modern history is meaningless, that no one country can be considered to the exclusion of the rest. The French, British, German, Spanish, and Italian populations, with their outlying appendages,

must for the purpose of this examination be regarded as members of one and the same political
whole.  The general laws of modern progress are
not to be gathered from the history of England, of
Spain, or of any other single country.  Works written
on the principle of exclusive nationality, useful as
they may be as collections of material, have to the
student of the science of history something of the
character of provincial or parochial records.  Western
Europe must be regarded as a whole, united in
mediæval times by a common religious faith, united
no less in modern times by a uniform system of
industrial activity, of scientific study, and æsthetic
culture.

Taking then the destructive movement first, the
question before us will be, At what stage had this
movement arrived in the period before us, and what
advance was made in it during that period ?

The essential feature of the mediæval system,
that feature on which all its greatness depended, and
which marked an era in the progress of humanity,
was the separation of the temporal or secular from
the moral or spiritual power.  Under the old theo-
cracies, whether we look at the Jewish or the Pagan
world, there had been priests and there had been
kings, but the two powers were closely connected
and combined, and one of them was at the mercy of
the other.  Either the civil magistrate, as in ancient
Rome, usurped the functions of the priest, or, as in
ancient Egypt, the priests usurped the office of the
magistrate, and regulated the civil government, or at
least the secular occupations of the people.  The
essential feature of Catholic society was, that a

power arose, for the first time in history, wholly independent of and disconnected from the State. From the time that the early Christians obeyed their bishops and disobeyed their magistrates ; from the time that St. Ambrose, from the threshold of his church in Milan, forbade the entrance of Theodosius, the supreme magistrate of the civilized world, because he came there stained with unlawful and unrepented massacre, it was evident that a new power had arisen among men ; a power acting by other laws than those of force, measuring by another standard than that of kingly favour or aristocratic birth. Charlemagne recognised that power as superior to his own imperial dignity. Henry IV recognised it when he sued for pardon barefoot at Hildebrand's gate. It was by the power of the Catholic Church antagonizing and balancing the rude force of feudalism, that the condition of the labouring classes was made tolerable. For the first time in the history of the world, the moral law was separated from the civil law ; the law of conscience and duty from the law of judicial ordinance and magisterial compulsion ; the law persuading the will from the law compelling the action. The Church wholly separate from and superior to the State ; binding the feudal States of Europe into a vast commonwealth, a spiritual democracy, where intellectual and moral force took precedence of birth, office, wealth, and regal power : such was the ideal partially realized between the tenth and the thirteenth century. Partially realized, I say, for at no time was the separation between Church and State so perfect as the theory of Catholicism indicated. Fully to have attained its

high ends, the power of that Church should have
been not less than it was, but greater. The Church,
in her best days, was the safeguard of spiritual
liberty against feudal oppression; but in its best
days it was too weak for the task, and those days
were far too short. The intellectual basis on which
it rested was too incoherent; it was impotent to
withstand the irresistible march of metaphysical and
scientific thought, finding utterance in Abelard, in
Roger Bacon, and in Dante; it was powerless to
deal with the nascent feature of the modern time,
the problem of free industry then rising in the
emancipated boroughs; and two centuries before
the days of Luther and of Calvin, the disruption of
Catholicism began. The subjection of the Papal
power to the power of Councils, the triumph of the
kings over the popes in the long and vital struggle
of ecclesiastical appointments, were the sure signs
that the life of the Catholic Church as a separate
and independent modifying force was gone for ever.

And in consequence of its fall the power of
feudalism would have been intolerable to the human
race, had not feudalism itself been undergoing a
similar decline; had not a new element of prodigious
significance, destined wholly to supersede feudalism,
been rising to take its place. That element was the
growth of free industry in the boroughs of Western
Europe during the eleventh, twelfth, and thirteenth
centuries. Not only were the free burghers the rivals
of the feudal power, but by the very mode in which
they obtained their freedom, they decomposed and
undermined that power. Of the two elements of
which the feudal power consisted, royalty and

aristocracy, they allied themselves with one, to the inevitable ruin, sooner or later, of the other. But the mode in which they did so was not the same in every European country ; and in the clear under-standing of the distinction lies the key to the important differences which, amidst still more im-portant and essential uniformities, demarcate the history of France from the history of England. In England, the burghers, the *tiers-état*, united with the aristocracy against the kings ; in France, it united with royalty against aristocracy. The explanation as to England may perhaps be sought in the peculiar circumstances of the Norman Conquest. There the monarchical element of feudalism was exceptionally strong ; there too there was a quasi-feudal element, that of the small Saxon gentry, who, sharing the oppression of their countrymen in the towns, shared their resistance, and were ultimately joined by the great barons. Hence the peculiar character of the English constitution : aristocratic rather than monarchic, provincial rather than metropolitan, localized not centralized. From Runnymede to the aristocratic appropriation of Church property at the dissolution of the monasteries, from the dissolution of the monasteries to the aristocratic Revolution of 1688, the power of the great landowning families in England relatively to the monarchy has been, with the tacit consent of the English people, ever on the increase ; and at the death of William III these families became virtually supreme, and the monarch, as has been well said, was reduced to the condition of the Venetian Doge.

In France, from inverse causes, the process was

inverse. There, in the eleventh and twelfth centuries, the feudal nobility was very strong, the monarchy singularly weak ; and there the Third Estate made common cause with the monarchy against the aristocratic power. Hence the different colour of subsequent French history. In France, in England, and in every other country of Europe, the ultimate goal was, and still remains—for it is as yet far from completely attained,—the same : the elimination of feudalism, of privileged classes, the full establishment of the modern system of free industry, the complete incorporation of the working classes into the political body. But whereas in England the people, in their progress towards this goal, have accepted the government of a strong provincial local aristocracy, depressing the feudal monarchy, and more or less effectually heading the industrial movement ; in France the people have co-operated with the monarchy against the aristocracy. For the French people, the growth of the monarchy was for many centuries the standard, the true measure of political progress. With the growth of the monarchy, the growth of the Third Estate, that is, of the professional and commercial class, went hand in hand. By its means the aristocratic power in France gradually lost its influence and its vitality, while retaining the semblance of life, until little remained for the revolutionists of 1789 but to clear away the husk, and from beneath the débris of the Middle Ages reveal the young and puissant form of modern France. Therefore the steps by which the kings of France attained their vast centralizing power deserve more attention and respect than republican politicians

might at first sight be disposed to afford ; for the
progress of the French monarchy has been the
progress of the French people.

The first kings of the Capetian dynasty seemed
hardly to deserve the name.    They were but the
first in rank among a long list of feudal nobles, and
they were by no means the first in power.    Their
dominions were not nearly so large as the county of
Yorkshire.    The Dukes of Normandy, whether before
or after their English conquests, openly scorned
their ascendency.    South of the Loire, the powerful
principalities of Aquitaine and Languedoc hardly
recognised their existence.    To the country east of
the Meuse, the Saone, and the Rhone, that is, to the
provinces of Lorraine, Burgundy, Franche Comté,
Dauphiné, and Provence, France laid no claim
whatever ; those provinces in the division of the
Carlovingian empire having fallen to the German
empire, or to the kingdom of Italy ; and even west
of the Saone, the Counts of Champagne and Artois,
doing nominal homage, exercised practical sovereignty
within thirty miles of Paris.

But since the time of Julius Cæsar the tradition of
a central authority had never wholly died out in France.
The Carlovingian dynasty revived the tradition of the
Roman Empire.    The Capetian dynasty revived the
tradition of Charlemagne.    Every influence favoured
the movement.    The boroughs, as we have seen,
made common cause with the king, or, in other parts
of France, with the great suzerains, against the petty
tyranny of the small barons, and welcomed the
establishment of central courts of appeal, from which
nobles were gradually excluded, and in which

lawyers, men of their own class, became gradually
supreme.  The Church, with instinctive prescience
of the secret agitation of free thought rising from
the free boroughs, or wafted in subtle miasmata from
the East, began to feel its need of a strong secular
arm, abnegated its superiority to the temporal power,
and accepted the protection of a vigorous monarchy,
purchasing bare subsistence at the cost of independence
and morality.  The great Crusading expeditions
meantime wasted the wealth and blood of the military
caste, banished them for long years from the kingdom,
and left the pacific elements of society, the burghers
and the lawyers, free to organize their settled
government at home, and substitute Roman law for
barbarous Germanic custom.  One by one the great
fiefs were united to the French crown.  Normandy
in 1204, Toulouse in 1271, Champagne in 1285,
Dauphiné in 1349, Aquitaine in 1453, Burgundy in
1479, Provence in 1487, Brittany in 1491, yielded
to the gravitating influence which, during the disastrous period from the middle of the fourteenth to the
middle of the fifteenth century, had been neutralized
by the English wars and the desperate struggles of
the Burgundian house, but which resumed its intensity
under the eleventh Louis, one of the wisest, and,
popular prejudice apart, one of the most useful of
European statesmen.  The efforts of Louis le Gros,
of Suger, of Philip Augustus, and of Saint Louis, to
break down feudal anarchy and establish a common
authority and a uniform administration throughout
France, had relaxed under the house of Valois, who
had yielded to the aristocratic instinct of providing
rich appanages for their family.  John, in 1362, by

bequeathing the Duchy of Burgundy, which had escheated to the Crown, to his fourth son, Philip the Bold, founded a rival dynasty, which, by inter-marriage with the family of Flanders, became for a time the strongest throne in Europe, and paralysed the resistance of France to the English invader. It seemed for a time doubtful whether France was not destined to the political dispersion of Italy and Germany. This formidable danger, increased by the union of other feudal magnates with the house of Burgundy, veiling their instincts of self-preservation under the guise of a League for the Common Good, Louis XI met and crushed. Military ambition of the vulgar Napoleonic kind he had none ; his sole aim was to constitute the French nation, by removing the incubus which rendered its existence impos-sible—the feudal aristocracy. Thoroughly devoted to the industrial and commercial interests of the nation, looking on the frivolous etiquette of the nobles with undisguised scorn, assuming the dress, and frequenting the society of commoners, Louis XI was the true precursor of Richelieu, and the Re-volution.

The English student of French history will seek for the analogue of that in which, when reading his own annals, he has taken a deep, a just, though a somewhat exaggerated pride : a free permanent representative assembly. And, for the most part, he will seek in vain. There were indeed two institutions in France, one permanent, the other intermittent, either of which exercised, in its way, a check upon the central power, and seemed to contain germs capable of development into the English type of

government. These were the States-General and
the Parlement of Paris. The States-General, consisting of the three estates of nobles, clergy, and
commons, were assembled for the first time by
Philip le Bel in 1302, thirty-five years after the
first English Parliament had been called by Simon
de Montfort. The popular element in this body
was chosen by a system of double election, in the
first stage of which every free man in every city,
town, and village, took part ; the deputies so elected
assembled in the chief city of the district, and sent a
member to the metropolis. It was convoked at rare
intervals in the fourteenth, fifteenth, and sixteenth centuries : it was called together by the Queen Regent
in 1614, but from that time it was not heard of,
until, after an interval of 170 years, it was again
convoked to inaugurate the French Revolution.
That these assemblies acted as a check upon expenditure, and as a safety-valve for discontent, is
unquestionable. They kept alive the old theory, a
theory far older than is imagined, that freemen
could not be taxed without their own consent.
They nursed the germ of modern republicanism ;
the dogma which has its roots deeper in the past
than is generally thought, and is therefore the more
certain of the future, that the common welfare of the
people, *res publica*, is the sole test by which the acts
of Government are to be judged, the sole object to
which they are to be directed. 'To the people,'
said Philippe Pot, in the States-General of 1484,
'and to the people alone, it belongs to determine
any question affecting the welfare of the commonwealth at large ; the government of it has been

confided to our kings by the people, and they who
have possessed themselves of it by any other means
than the consent of the people, are nothing less than
tyrants and usurpers. The king being unable to
govern the State in his own person, the government
reverts to the people, from whom he received it. By
the people I do not mean the populace, or merely
the commons of the realm, but all Frenchmen of
every condition.' Let it be owned at once that
these principles were boldly enunciated only at rare
intervals, and were most imperfectly put in practice ;
let it be owned that, in the sixteenth, seventeenth,
and eighteenth centuries, the French monarchs, with
or without the advice of men of note in the provinces, whom they called to their counsels, voted
their own budgets, checked only by the passive
resistance of the second institution to which I have
referred : the judicial courts, otherwise called Parlements, of Paris and of the Southern Provinces. The
contrast in this vital question of taxation between
France and England seems at first sight extreme.
Further examination will, I think, diminish the force
of that contrast. The theory that the consent of
the people was necessary to taxation has existed on
either side of the Channel. But in neither has it
been carried into practice. The practical government of France has been a strong centralized
monarchy administered by middle-class officials.
The practical government of England has been an
equally strong local aristocracy, administered by
aristocratic officials. Popular consent to taxation
during the last three centuries has been the rule in
neither, as in England assuredly it is not the rule

C

now.[1]   And whether the Government be a united
monarchy, or a commercial and feudal aristocracy,
whether the millions be governed by the thousands,
or be governed by one, would seem to be to the
millions, however it may seem to the thousands, a
matter of but secondary importance.

The centralizing, nationalizing, anti-feudal process,
carried on so successfully by the eleventh Louis, met
with serious checks during the sixteenth century ;
partly from the insane ambition of Francis I and his
successor to found a power in Italy, partly from the
disturbances produced by the religious wars.   I
shall have occasion to speak of the Protestant
question in a subsequent lecture, from the religious
or ecclesiastical point of view.   At present, we are
concerned only with the political disunion which it
produced.   In two ways, it promoted a revival of
the feudal spirit.   The great mass of the French
people held aloof from the Protestant movement
altogether.   To Paris especially, it was utterly
repugnant.   It took root in a certain number of
the smaller towns ; but by no class was it so
eagerly welcomed as by the aristocracy and gentry.
By the Edict of Nantes, the Protestant worship was
licensed in 3,500 castles.   The Condés, the Châtillons,
the Lesdiguières, the Rosnys, the Rohans, the
Duplessis-Mornays, the Colignys, and countless others,
illustrate the aristocratic character of French Protestantism.   Had the French reformers carried the
day, as before the day of St. Bartholomew seemed

---

[1] [These lectures were published, it must be remembered, in 1866.
The electoral basis of England has been profoundly modified since then
by the Reform Acts of 1867 and 1884.]

hardly impossible, a new impulse would have been
given to feudalism in France; local aristocratic
government would have taken the place of centralized
middle-class government.    Had this been the result,
not merely the resistance of France to the over-
bearing power of the Austro-Spanish monarchy
would have been weakened, but the progress of
French thought would have been hampered, and the
great philosophical movement of the last century
culminating in the French Revolution would have
been very seriously retarded.    Again, those among
the great feudal families of France who sided with
the old religion, took advantage of the confusion of
the time to assert the federative feudal principle.
At the extinction of the house of Valois, Henry IV,
the first of the Bourbons, found arrayed against him
the celebrated league of great nobles, whose avowed
objects were not merely to crush the Reformation,
to promote in every way the extreme Catholic
reaction, and to place the French throne at the mercy
of the Spanish monarchy, but, above all, to restore
feudalism in France by making their own governments in the provinces perpetual and hereditary.
This, indeed, was the one grand object of the
French aristocracy, whether Catholic or Protestant.
After the government of Henry IV had been
secured, after the settlement of the nation and the
equilibrium of religions had been established, the
very nobles who had supported the king turned
against him ; and the insatiate desire of perpetuating
their feudal power, by establishing hereditary government in their provinces, gave rise to a most formidable conspiracy, headed by the man who had passed

himself for the king's most intimate personal friend, the Marshal de Biron.  The avowed policy of these conspirators, for which they did not scruple to call in the assistance of the Spanish government, was to assimilate the condition of France to the condition of Germany ; to establish themselves in their provincial governments, with a nominal allegiance to the king, not more onerous than that by which the princes of the empire were bound to the Austrian sovereign.

Needless to say, that had such miserable policy been successful, the power of France, as the centre of the great European commonwealth, would have been nullified.  There would have been left no power in Europe capable of resisting the Catholic reaction inaugurated by the Spanish monarchy, and maintained by the Austrian empire ; and the Thirty Years' War would have had a result widely different from that equilibrium of States and of Religions, which it is the great glory of Richelieu, as the organ of the French monarchy, to have obtained.  Uniformly from the fourteenth century to the eighteenth, has the policy of the French nobility been self-seeking, anti-national, and retrograde ; almost as uniformly from the fourteenth century to the seventeenth, has the policy of the French monarchy been centralizing, anti-feudal, and coincident with the common interests of the French nation and of Europe.

Henry IV, one of the noblest types among progressive statesmen, availed himself of his high position, as one of the founders of French national unity, to do all that lies within the sphere of a ruler to facilitate the downfall of the old system, to encourage the formation of the new. In France, he strove, and strove successfully, against feudal tyranny ; and with the aid of his great minister, Sully, he devoted the whole energies of the State to the removal of shackles upon industry and commerce ; to the equalization, so far as was then possible, of taxation ; to the encouragement of new branches of industry ; to the formation of transatlantic colonies. In Europe, he grasped more clearly than any former statesman the conception of the Commonwealth of Western nations ; and looked forward, it may be with too Utopian a gaze, to the prospect, which to us is no longer Utopian, of a common European arbitration, of an universal Peace. Practically, he set every engine in motion for uniting with the Protestant powers of Northern Europe for resistance to the common enemy of progress, the retrograde monarchies of Austria and of Spain.

Death cut short his great designs ; the government of the Queen Regent, feeble, unprincipled, and unscrupulous, threw his noble projects to the winds, married the heir to the throne into the Spanish house, and appeased the grasping selfishness of the feudal lords by scandalous and enormous bribes. But at that critical period in French history arose one of those few men to whom it is given to modify very largely the life of humanity, to accelerate the speed of progress, and hasten the advent of a more perfect civilisation. That man was Armand Duplessis, Bishop of Luçon, afterwards better known as Cardinal de Richelieu. A clerical representative at the States-General of 1614, he attracted the attention of the Queen Regent, and under her auspices rose to office. The helpless confusion produced by an incompetent administration prepared the way for him. Louis XIII, not void of insight, not without a sense of duty, but timid, melancholy, frivolous, pietistic, equally unambitious and incapable of power, handed over the helm to the man whose fitness it is his great credit to have recognised; and from 1618 to 1642, Richelieu was the sole dictator of France.

Of his European policy we shall speak afterwards; it was animated by the same wise spirit, conservative and yet progressive, that moulded his policy at home. To constitute the French republic, to reach that ideal government where all the forces of the State should be directed to the common welfare——an ideal towards which the French Revolution of 1789 made the greatest stride that has ever yet been taken by men,——it was necessary first to constitute the French monarchy, and to that object he bent the powers of his unswerving and relentless will.

Between him and his ideal stood one great obstacle. A few thousand families, scattered over every province in France, advanced claims with which the existence either of a strong monarchy or of a true republic were wholly incompatible. They claimed to belong to a superior caste; they lived in castellated mansions, where they administered justice and the game-laws to the peasantry of their district; forced the peasant proprietor (for even in those days there were peasant proprietors in France) to grind his corn at their mill, to crush his grapes at their winepress, to pay what tolls they pleased when he crossed their river. From all taxation, except from that small portion which was levied on imports and by means of excise, this class claimed entire exemption, their duties to the king being, as they said, sufficiently performed by their military service. Above all, they asserted absolute possession of a very large portion of the soil of France, and claimed feudal dues, amounting to a heavy rent-charge upon the rest ; they monopolized all appointments in the army and navy, and claimed most of the higher appointments in the civil service ; the highest appointments of all, those of governors of provinces, they perseveringly endeavoured to secure as an hereditary possession in their families.

Such was one of the great obstacles that stood between Richelieu and the French republic. Such was French feudalism in the beginning of the seventeenth century ; widely different, it will be seen, from the feudalism of five centuries before, when the system, rude, barbarous, and imperfect as it was, was yet instinct with life ; when serfage was recognised, as in the so-called free republics of Greece and Rome slavery had been recognised, as the natural normal condition of the labouring class ; when the homage of the tenant to the lord, of the lord to the suzerain, expressed subordination without servility, superiority without contempt ; when the feudal castle was a camp of refuge for the villagers who clustered under its walls ; when the possession of the soil was not, as in modern times, an absolute possession, but held as a civil function, involving military duties, defence of the kingdom, defence of Christendom against Paganism ; and when abuse of these great powers—abuse of them being far too frequent,—was checked by a strong and thoroughly organized spiritual power, recruited from the lowest as well as from the highest ranks, owning another allegiance, recognising a higher standard ; widely different, I say, from the mediæval feudalism was the corrupt and spurious feudalism of France in the seventeenth century ; feudalism without the necessities and without the duties which from the ninth century to the thirteenth had justified, mitigated, and ennobled its existence.

Such was the great obstacle that stood between Richelieu and the French republic. He removed it, not wholly, but partially. Much was left for the States-General of 1789 ; the celebrated 4th of August found vast masses of wreck and refuse to sweep away ; the great men of the Convention consolidated the work, which, under the usurped name of the Code Napoléon, still stands as a model for the legislators of Europe. But of these great reformers, Richelieu was the principal forerunner. Speaking broadly, it may be said that he destroyed utterly the political vitality of feudalism ; its social influence he destroyed less completely. The means he used were not such as would have satisfied the modern democrat. But they were, I believe, the most efficacious, the only efficacious means for his time and his purpose. He destroyed the political power of the French aristocracy, by largely increasing the power of the French monarchy. The method which, on the supposition that he was sincerely desirous for the public well-being, most English politicians will consider that he ought to have adopted, Richelieu did not adopt. He never summoned the States-General. He adopted no form whatever of elective representation ; nor did he increase the political power of the great judicial body, which had on several occasions assumed constitutional functions : the Parlement of Paris. In Richelieu's eyes, Parliamentary government, as applied to the France of the seventeenth century (it is doubtful whether, in other ages and in other countries, it has frequently been otherwise), implied the political supremacy of the very class against whose influence he was contending, the supremacy of the great landholders. And even supposing that he could have infused into the States-General a somewhat larger proportion of the middle-class element, of the leading commercial capitalists, yet the government of a feudal and commercial aristocracy, the government of the poor by the rich without any counterpoising check, which exists[1] in our own country at the present time, and which various efforts have been made to introduce into France and other continental countries, was not precisely the ideal of Richelieu. Government by States-General, a body in which the two privileged estates of clergy and nobility neutralized the action of the Third Estate, would simply have provoked that intestine dissension, which, during the religious wars of the sixteenth, or in the English wars of the fourteenth century, had proved so favourable to aristocratic tyranny. By strengthening the monarchy in France, he promoted the welfare even of the French bourgeoisie, but above all, that of the

[1] [It is well to remind readers again that these lectures were published in 1866.]

great mass of the working population in town or country, far more effectually than by a fractional increase of the plebeian minority in the States-General. Feudalism in the hands of Richelieu was concentrated into a single institution, hereditary monarchy ; and by this concentration not only were its intrinsic evils diminished, but its final disappearance in the succeeding century was materially facilitated.

It must be added, that in the prosecution of this trenchant and destructive policy, he was singularly aided by the contemptible character of the men with whom he had to deal. At the death of Henry IV, in 1610, the great princes of the kingdom advanced formidable claims to partition the government of the kingdom among themselves, and to found an hereditary oligarchy after the English or Venetian type. Disastrous as concession to their claim would have been, the ambition that prompted them was in no way strange. What was strange and more than usually despicable was, that they should so readily have consented to barter their claims for money. The feeble ministers of the first years of Louis XIII, in order to carry on the king's government at all, were forced to dissipate the resources which the wisdom of Sully had economized. The first princes of France, men like the Prince of Condé, or the Count of Soissons, took large sums in cash, or pensions of £20,000 a year, as the price for which they would consent to abstain from troubling the peace of the kingdom. And this was a fair sample of their political morality. Every virtue, except that of personal courage, seemed to have utterly deserted them. In statesmanlike views, in the sympathies of the citizen, in the elementary sense of patriotism

owned by the starving and illiterate peasant, they
were wholly wanting. They were the true progenitors
of the emigrant and traitorous noblesse of the Revolution. They were always ready to barter away their
country's freedom to the Spaniard, and to barter it
at a very low price.

There was but one way of dealing with such men.
If France was to be governed with a strong hand,
these men must be crushed with an iron heel. The
eighteen years of Richelieu's dictatorship are occupied
with a perpetual series of mischievous conspiracies
against the king's government, and of treasonable
negotiations with Spain, in which the Montmorencys,
the Condés, the Soissons, the Épernons were the
chief traitors. Richelieu's course was wise, merciful,
and inflexibly severe. He struck the chief traitors
and these alone. When he enforced his laws against
duelling, it was a Montmorency whom he chose for
his example ; when he wished to strike terror in the
crew of malversators of the public money, it was
a Marshal de Marillac whom he sent to the scaffold.
The list of the defendants in his State trials suffices
to show this. Forty-seven sentences of death for
political offences were pronounced during his reign.
Among those who suffered we find five dukes, four
counts, a marshal of France, and the king's special
favourite and grand equerry Cinq-Mars. Most of the
rest were nobles, though of lower rank.[1] Of these
forty-seven sentences, twenty-six only were actually
put in force ; a number which is far less than the
loud cries uttered against Richelieu's tyranny have

[1] See authorities quoted in *Les fondateurs de l'Unité Française* by
Count Louis de Carné, vol. ii, p. 300.

led historians to imagine.    That each of these
twenty-six men was guilty of high treason ten
times over, treason unpalliated by a single worthy
motive, was not and could not be denied.    But the
shrieks of expiring feudalism were loud and long ;
and Richelieu's name was cursed by the aristocracy
of France, until Danton supplied another and more
formidable object for their curses.

But Richelieu did not content himself with deci-
mating the French nobility.    He undermined and
overthrew their political power.    The provinces into
which France was divided before the Revolution, had
been entrusted by the French kings to the government of some leading noblemen, whose position
within the province was as important as that of the
Viceroy of Ireland before the Union, and who per-
petually endeavoured to make that position hereditary
in their family.    Richelieu undermined the power of
these provincial governors by substituting a rival
power more adapted to the practical exigencies of
government.    He placed in each province an Intendant, with powers much resembling those of a
Prefect of Department under the Second Empire ;
powers directly derived from the Privy Council.
These Intendants were invariably men of the middle
class, usually lawyers ;  their salary was moderate,
their social position by no means high.    But they
were always men of energy and ability, and gradually
the whole work of assessing the taxation and of
internal administration was transferred to their hands.
The system of Intendants was one of the most
direct steps taken by pre-revolutionary France in the
direction of centralized Republicanism.

Again, Richelieu found the soil of France, as has
been already observed, covered with innumerable
feudal castles. The men who held these castles,
holding them nominally for the king's service, were
not likely to be very docile subjects or orderly
citizens. Their demolition was essential to public
order, and Richelieu demolished them without mercy.
In 1626 he held in Paris one of those assemblies of
Notables, which served him instead of a Parliament ;
an assembly of twelve bishops, twelve lords, none of
them belonging to the higher nobility, and twenty-
nine lawyers or finance officers. These men were all
elected by himself ; and he submitted for their advice
some of the most important questions of government.
That they were not a servile body of court-sycophants
is proved by the opposition they offered to some of
his most cherished projects, which, in accordance
with their wishes, were postponed. But in the
question of castle-demolition, they were entirely at
one with him. On their suggestion, and on that of
the local assemblies of Brittany and other provinces,
it was decreed that all castles not necessary as
frontier - fortresses should forthwith be dismantled.
Five of these fortresses were demolished in Poitou,
two in Dauphiné ; and this is a fair specimen of
what was done elsewhere. All fortification of private
houses was henceforth forbidden.

Thus it was that this great statesman advanced
the great destructive movement of modern history ;
and by the downfall of the Feudal system prepared
the way for the Republican polity, founded upon
peaceful industry, which was inaugurated by the
Revolution of 1789, and which it is the infamy of

the first Napoleon to have retarded. I have given but an imperfect sketch of his internal policy. I have not yet described his dealings with French Calvinism, the political power of which, grown dangerous to peaceful government, he narrowly restricted, while leaving its civil liberty intact. Nor have I yet spoken of his European diplomacy, of the masterly firmness with which he guided the helm of Europe, calmed the fierce and fruitless struggle of Protestant and Catholic, and organized that equilibrium of Western States, to which, though temporary, the order and the progress of the last two centuries are in great part due. His ideal, like that of all great men, outstripped the realized result. Those who would appreciate the full nobility of his aim must read his *Political Testament.* That masterpiece of wisdom, under its antique and monarchical forms of language, testifies to his deep devotion to the welfare of France ; to his strong desire to lighten her taxation, especially the taxation of her peasantry ; to his strenuous efforts to forward her commercial and industrial greatness. Hated by the nobility, mistrusted by the clergy, misunderstood by large masses of his countrymen, his life, worn down for the last ten years of it by hopeless and incurable disease, and threatened every moment by a long series of assassins, hung always as by a hair on the life of the nominal king, himself a helpless invalid, who survived him but a few months. Hating him much, fearing him more, and respecting him most of all, Louis XIII never yielded to the court flatterers, who hungered for the death of both. It was a tragic and heroic struggle with great problems and miserable foes, with obstinate meanness, pertinacious treachery, and the worst of all tyrannies, the tyranny of the weak. Death came before his prime of power was past, but not before his work was done. Those who stood by his deathbed, we are told, were astonished at his calmness. Their purblind eyes looked in vain for traces of a troubled conscience, of blood-stained memories. They judged him by their own standard, and supposed that he would never have given himself the trouble to contend with traitors, except for the paltry ambition of supplanting them. They asked him if he forgave his enemies. The dying man's thoughts were far away in the future of Europe and of France. ' I have had no enemies,' he replied, ' except the enemies of the State.' [1]

His death was followed within a few months by that of Louis XIII. His son, Louis XIV, was but five years old. Anne of Austria, his mother, daughter of Philip III of Spain, assumed the regency. During her husband's life she had been the soul of the aristocratic opposition. She had been constantly engaged in treasonable correspondence with Spain. Richelieu had been her avowed and relentless enemy. But not many months after she had felt the weight and responsibility of government, she is reported to have stopped for a few minutes before a masterpiece of Philippe de Champagne, which all who have visited the gallery of the Louvre should know well, the portrait of the great Cardinal. She looked for a few moments at that massive brow, the clear-cut Dantesque face, so expressive of high culture, profound

---

[1] *Memoirs of Madame de Motteville* (1723, Amsterdam), vol. i, p. 115.

thought, and imperial resolve ; then, turning to her
attendant, said : ' If that man were living, he would
be first minister of France still.' [1]     Certain it is, at
least, that she took into her counsels the man who
had been trained by Richelieu, and whom he had
avowedly put forward for his successor, Giulio
Mazarini ; and that from that time forward she
accepted the monarchical and national traditions of
Richelieu, rejecting the policy of the aristocratic and
anti-national clique that surrounded her.

Such, then, was the French monarchy in the
middle of the seventeenth century.    It was an
institution of vast power for good and for evil.    It
originated in the decay of the Papal power in the
thirteenth and fourteenth centuries, in the necessity
of a strong government to preserve at least material
order amidst the disruption of the Catholic system,
in the alliance of the kings with the new elements of
society, the bourgeoisie and the civil lawyers, against
the retrograde ecclesiastical and feudal elements.
The later founders of the monarchy, Louis XI,
Henry IV, and Richelieu, had seen, each with
greater clearness than the last, the true character of
the institution.    Rightly used, it was an agency of
vast power for sweeping away the ruined elements
of the old structure of society, and for developing
the germs of the new structure founded on peaceful
industry and free mental growth.    Peace abroad and
order at home were the obvious conditions of such
development ; and peace and order had been the
objects of these great statesmen.    Viewed thus, the
French monarchy was a sort of dictatorship, necessary

---

[1] Martin, *Histoire de France*, vol. xi, p. 590.

for a few generations, to preserve material order in the midst of utter confusion of beliefs and ideas, until some new spiritual order should arise, which should render the necessity for any such concentration of material power unnecessary. Of such dictators the great Frederick of Prussia has been in modern times the most perfect type. Had Richelieu been succeeded by such a man, had Louis XIV been somewhat less fatally inferior to him, the final disappearance of feudalism in the eighteenth century would indeed not have been delayed. The French Revolution would have come ; but the horrors of the French Revolution would have been spared. Aristocracy and hereditary Monarchy would have been swept away none the less ; and the Republicanism of modern France would have arisen, as it has arisen, in their place ; but the substitution would have taken place without the convulsion, and without the bitterness.

These things at the point we have now reached, the minority of Louis XIV, still hang doubtful. Will the monarchy henceforth side frankly, as it has hitherto sided, with the *tiers état*, leaving Feudalism and Catholicism to their natural process of decay ? Or will a conservative reaction set in ; will an attempt be made to dam up the torrent of modern progress, and to rebuild the old ruins upon some quicksand which it has not yet swept away ? The torrent will find its issue, of this we may be sure, in either case ; but in the one event there will be peaceful establishment of the modern era ; in the other there will be a Second of September, a Reign of Terror, and a long series of retrograde wars.

D

# LECTURE II

FIVE years before the death of Richelieu, the first
of the two sons of Anne of Austria was born. His
father survived the great Cardinal only a few months,
and the seventy-two years of the reign of Louis XIV
now begin. In the present Lecture I propose to
continue the subject of the internal government of
France under the two great successors of Richelieu,
Mazarin and Colbert.

As Gustavus Adolphus bequeathed to Europe a
school of great soldiers, so Richelieu had gathered
round him a still more eminent school of great
diplomatists ; and meditating, as he must have
meditated, so frequently upon the future of France
and of Europe, when his own fragile life should have
been shattered, he fixed upon one of these to succeed
him in the government of France. That successor
was an Italian and an ecclesiastic, Giulio Mazarini.
Thoroughly versed in all the complex details of
Italian diplomacy, he had attracted the Cardinal's
notice in the negotiations between the Spanish and
French armies in the Duchy of Mantua twelve years
before, on which occasion he had been attached to

34

the Papal embassy. Richelieu had brought him into the French Foreign Office, and his twelve years' training under such consummate guidance had made him thoroughly master of the details of European diplomacy, and of the large progressive policy of his predecessor.

A greater contrast between the two statesmen can hardly be conceived. Stern, inflexible, massive, far-reaching, profound, pitiless, Richelieu could hardly have felt much personal sympathy for the wily, supple, adroit, fair-spoken man to whom he transmitted his power. But Richelieu knew his man, and knew the work which was cut out for him. The task of his own life had been twofold : the internal process of crushing the French aristocracy and founding the French monarchy upon its ruins ; the external work, which is to be explained in the next Lecture, of humbling the retrograde powers of Austria and Spain, and of carrying out the policy which found its issue in the treaties of Westphalia and the Pyrenees. Of these two tasks, the first was thoroughly accomplished, the second was incomplete. For the first, Mazarin would have been wholly incompetent ; his foreign blood, his alien manner, his ridiculous Italian accent, his physical timidity, would have utterly disqualified him for such warfare as Richelieu waged against the proud, polished, insolent, and unscrupulous aristocracy of mediæval France. As a master of the diplomatic art, he was hardly second to Richelieu himself ; but as an internal administrator, as the representative of the central power against feudal anarchy and lawless aristocratic pretension, he would have been wholly incompetent

had not the work been so effectually done before
him.

As it was, his want of experience in the details
of internal government, his incapacity to understand
the French nature, and, it must be added, his
deficient uprightness and firmness, counted for much
in the partial success of that somewhat contemptible
revolution which, owing to the literary skill of its
chief actors, rather than to its intrinsic importance,
has become immortalized as the insurrection of the
Fronde.    So much has been said and written about
this crisis, that it is desirable to form a due measure
of its importance.

Let us understand, then, that between the years
1648 and 1652, a last attempt was made by the
French noblesse to regain their lost influence, to
establish themselves as feudal hereditary princes in
their separate provinces, to undo the work of
Louis XI, of Henry IV, and of Richelieu, and thus to
nullify the influence of the only power in Europe
that could resist the retrograde pressure of Austria
and Spain.    But paralysed and decimated as they
had been by Richelieu, the noblesse by themselves
were incapable even of initiating such an enterprise.
Attempting the tactics that, ever since Magna
Charta, have proved so successful in the hands of the
aristocracy of England, they made, or pretended to
make, common cause with the upper ranks of the
middle classes, and cloaked their frivolous ambition
under the specious veil of the grievances of the Parlement of Paris.

It needs hardly to be mentioned, that between
the Parlement of Paris and the Long Parliament

then sitting in London there was little resemblance
but the name.   Sprung from the same stock, the
two institutions had in the interval between the
thirteenth and seventeenth centuries become widely
differentiated.   The Parlement of Paris, like that
of England, was originally the Privy Council of
the King, formed of his chief barons.   Louis IX,
in the thirteenth century, modified its purely feudal
character by the introduction of twenty lawyers as
secretaries.   The feudal element gradually disappeared ;   these secretaries gradually became the
acting members of the body, and were constituted
as the Supreme Court of Appeal from all Courts
in France, except those of the outlying provinces,
such as Brittany, Languedoc, and Burgundy, where
similar Courts existed.   In the fourteenth century
the members of this Supreme Court were appointed
for life ;   subsequently they were allowed to elect
new members into their body ;   and, under the reign
of Henry IV, their office, subject to a tax of 2
per cent upon the income, became virtually trans-
missible to their descendants, or might be sold, like
appointments in the English army, to any properly
qualified purchaser.   It was a system inherently
defective and liable to glaring abuses, of which the
statesmen of that day were perfectly well aware ;
but it had at least the compensating advantage of
keeping the judicial power in France free from
undue pressure on the part of the executive ;   and
to it perhaps, are in part due the high character,
the uprightness, and the independence which, even
under the most absolute and oppressive régimes, have
always honourably distinguished the French bar.

But, in addition to their judicial functions, the
Parlement of Paris had gradually acquired a certain
political prestige, which, during the troublous period
of the Calvinistic wars, tended to become a political
power.    As the secretaries of the King's Privy
Council, it was their duty to register his edicts ; the
consultative voice which, as members of that council,
was readily granted them, was apt, under weak
monarchs, to become loud and louder in its tone ;
and the theory softly whispered under a Sully or
a Richelieu, was boldly broached under their feeble
successors, that, until the king's edicts were registered
by Parlements, they had not the force of law.    By
simply declining or delaying to register in their rolls
an edict of taxation, this Supreme Court of Law
could interpose an indefinite and irregular, but sometimes a very effective check to unreasonable expenditure.    And thus it was that, utterly different in
character, in constitution, in purpose, as was the
Parlement of Paris from the Parliament of West-
minster, it fell out that in the middle of the seventeenth century both institutions were using analogous
weapons for analogous purposes ; and that this self-
elected body of lawyers, by declining to register
the king's budget, was advancing claims not less
formidable in appearance than those before which
the crown of England was destined to succumb.

' The first four years of the king's minority,' says
Cardinal de Retz, ' were tided over by the mere
swing which Richelieu had given to the progress
of the monarchical power.'    But then came the
struggle.    Twelve years of war had brought on a
financial crisis.    Extraordinary taxation became

necessary, and it was in their resistance to this taxation that the Supreme Law Courts of Paris came into collision with the monarchy.    The special bone of contention was the increase of the *Paulette*, the tax imposed during Henry IV's reign upon their salaries, and the imposition of which was the guarantee for their hereditary tenure of office.

It is worth while to glance for a moment as eye-witnesses into old Paris during the month of August in 1648 ; not forgetting that the King of England was in Carisbrooke prison then ; and that, in the year before, the Viceroy of Naples had yielded his power to a fisherman.    The loud debates in the old Palais de Justice ; the grave lawyers, who from time immemorial had been the bulwarks of the monarchical authority against the feudal power, goaded into hot opposition ; the Parlement making common cause with the other sovereign Courts of Paris ; Presidents Lamoignon, Talon, De Mesmes, Molé, strenuously attacking Mazarin's profligate expenditure with one hand, and with the other as strenuously pressing backward against Broussel, 'the Roman tribune,' and other impetuous members of their own body, who in antique classical republican harangues, were agitating for nothing less than a complete transference to themselves of the whole legislative power of the monarchy ; the people of Paris who, ever since the religious wars, had become a political power in France, with whom statesmen had to count,[1] hanging on the lips of these grave

[1] 'Un de nos Rois,' says Madame de Motteville (alluding to Henry III), 'a dit que cette tête du Royaume était trop grosse, qu'elle était pleine de beaucoup d'humeurs nuisibles au repos de ses membres; et que la saignée de temps en temps lui était nécessaire.'    She remarks

agitators, and clamouring for the removal of the *octroi* just imposed on all provisions brought into the city ; the noblesse, eagerly watching which party offered the best leverage for the restoration of their power ; the proud Austrian Queen, half insolent, half piteous of the people's misery, not unwilling, were it less troublesome, to alleviate their distress, but chiefly scandalized at their disobedience; Mazarin, her confidential minister (if not, as it was whispered, in a far nearer relation), the butt of that terrible Parisian sarcasm which, like the flash of the cannon, is so apt to be followed by its shot and shell, managing his foes and friends with smiling face and trembling heart, framing his hand-to-mouth budgets, amassing an enormous private fortune, yet never losing sight of that which alone redeems him, the high aim of his European diplomacy,—such was political life in Paris while the Thirty Years' War was being closed at Munster, Spanish armies alone standing stubbornly against young Condé in the Netherlands.

The drama, after all, would have hardly sufficient interest for us, but for the inimitable skill of its narrators, who, like insects in amber, have immortalized their own and their friends' littleness in the brilliant transparency of their French style. We have memoirs of a Mademoiselle de Montpensier, bravest and unbashfullest of Amazons, fighting and

---

in another place : ' Les émotions populaires dans Paris, qui est plutôt un Monde entier qu'une Ville particulière, sont des torrens furieux qui s'étendent avec une si grande impétuosité, que si on les laissait grossir, ils seraient capables de faire des ravages que la postérité par leurs terribles effets aurait peut-être de la peine à les croire.'—De Motteville, vol. i, p. 237, vol. ii, p. 276.

intriguing for a husband, royal, princely, ducal, or,
if better might not be, at least noble; of a Madame
de Motteville, Queen's favourite, sweet, faithful,
ladylike, the insolence of her caste and breeding
contrasting so strangely with the delicate gentleness
and candour of her nature; finally, of the Archbishop,[1] and arch-conspirator himself, John Francis
Paul de Gondi, afterwards Cardinal de Retz;
intriguing overnight with every disaffected man,
whether prince of the blood, parliamentary orator,
hungry trader, or starving artisan; moving the
market women to tears next morning, in the nave
of Notre Dame, by eloquent discourses on the duty
of forgiveness to enemies; haranguing the mob
from his coach, when the service was over, with
cautious, cunning, stimulating exhortations to obey
the Queen, and disobey her chosen minister; pre-
senting himself at Court in the afternoon with the
cool, shrewd audacity of a Parisian gamin, and
offering to quell the rioters; and finding leisure in
this busy life for scandalous intrigues with the most
fashionable ladies of the period; De Retz, bright-
eyed, impudent ecclesiastical demagogue, vicious,
witty, veracious hypocrite, has in his inimitable
memoirs left photographic images of all that passed
around him.

The excitement of Paris, and indeed in many
other large towns in France, was very great in these
months. War, famine, and misgovernment were
doing their work. Every class in society was
agitated. The aristocracy, resuscitated for a brief
moment from the death-blow dealt by Richelieu,

---

[1] More properly acting archbishop, or coadjutor, to his uncle.

and indulging to the full their busy frivolous ambition ; the bourgeoisie, unprepared for radical changes, but disgusted with extravagant expenditure and repudiation of State loans, amounting to national bankruptcy ; the members of the Parlement and other Courts, terrified at the creation of new offices, and the threatened suppression of their hereditary privileges ; the working classes maddened by the recent *octroi* on provisions : all these things made inflammable material enough. The Queen, going to mass one morning, was beset by two hundred starving women, who followed her into the church doors, and clamoured for justice. She told us, says Madame de Motteville, on her return, that she had half a mind to speak to them ; 'mais elle avait appréhendé les insolences de cette canaille qui n'écoutent jamais la raison et qui n'ont dans la tête que leur petit intérêt.'[1] The Advocate-General, Omer Talon, with speech more bold than courtly, in full Parlement, on the 15th of January, 1648, told her that she was the Queen, not of slaves, but of free subjects ; yet that these subjects were so loaded with subsidies and taxes that, if they could still call their souls their own, it was because it was the only thing left that could not be sold by auction ; that laurels and glorious victories were well, but that, once for all, they were not food and clothing.[2]

The Parlement was the sheet-anchor of all men's hopes. They united in June, with the other supreme Courts, and sat permanently in the Salle de St. Louis. The pressure which they were bringing to bear on the Government seemed likely to be effectual ;

---

[1] De Motteville, vol. ii, p. 11.         [2] *Ibid.* p. 14.

checks on taxation and a Habeas Corpus law were already in progress, when, on the 19th of August, the news came of Condé's victory over the Spanish at Lens. The Court was in exultation. 'How sorry the Parlement will be!'[1] said Louis, now ten years old, and already accustomed, Madame de Motteville tells us, to look on the Parlement as his enemies.

Against these enemies the Court now resolved to strike a decisive blow. On the 26th of August, the Queen went to Notre Dame to hear the *Te Deum* for her victory; as she left it, she whispered to Cominges, the lieutenant of her guards, orders to seize the three leaders of the Parlementary opposition; foremost among them Broussel, the people's idol, an elderly man, 'the Roman tribune,' simple, upright, noisy, and unwise. How Cominges seized this 'tribune of the people' at his dinner-table, and put him struggling into his coach; how the coach was overturned, chains stretched across the streets, and the prisoner all but rescued, but at last got safely to St. Germain; the terror of the courtiers; the Queen brave and ignorant; crushing with ironical replies the impudent De Retz, who offers his services to quell the tumult, and is answered only by a 'Pray, don't put yourself to such trouble, sir,'—'Allez vous reposer, vous avez bien travaillé,' laughing heartily at good, gentle De Motteville, who naïvely confesses her fright; these, and other things, those who like good French and good comedy may read in the memoirs as with the very eyes and ears of the chief actors. Very soon

[1] De Motteville, vol. ii, p. 238.

the comedy seemed likely to become tragic enough ;
all night the streets were hushed with dismay and
expectation, but at six o'clock next morning, as
Séguier, the Chancellor of France, was proceeding
along the Quai des Augustins, with orders from the
Court to shut the doors of the Palais de Justice
against the Parlement, a band of armed citizens
incited, De Retz tells us, by himself, with their leader,
Argenteuil, in the disguise of a journeyman mason,
attacked the Swiss Guard, drove the Chancellor
into the courtyard of the house nearest at hand,
followed him there, and would assuredly have torn
him to pieces, but for a small closet into which
he managed to creep, and where it may well be
believed, says De Motteville, that as he heard the
crowd hustling and hunting for him in every
corner, he could not have felt very comfortable,
and must have felt that after all he was but a man
like the rest (qu'il n'était pas à son aise, et qu'il
sentit qu'il était homme). He confessed himself,
she goes on to add, while in this closet, to his
brother the Bishop of Meaux, and in every way
prepared himself for death. Paris meantime had
blazed out into full rebellion. The train had caught
fire, and every quarter of the city was exploding.
Never in after times were those two startling features
of Parisian outbreaks, instantaneous contagion and
instinctive organization, more signally displayed.
'Every one,' says Retz, 'without exception, took
up arms. We saw children of five or six years old
with daggers in their hand ; we saw mothers putting
them into their hands themselves. In less than two
hours there were more than twelve hundred barri-

cades, girt with banners and with weapons of all
sorts left from the old days of the League. I saw
in the Rue Neuve Notre-Dame, a little lad of eight
or ten years dragging, rather than carrying, a lance
which certainly must have come from the old
English wars. One man carried about an image
of the monk who killed Henry III, with the inscrip-
tion, " Long live St. Jacques Clement !" This I
ordered to be broken, amid shouts on all sides of
" Long live the King !" and echoing answers, " Down
with Mazarin !" '

The barricades remained standing all that day.
There was panic in the Court, and last of all that
panic reached the Queen. To the cries of the
people, ' Give us back our Broussel !' enforced by
deputation after deputation from the Parlement, she
replied by sullen refusal or irritated menace ; till at
length, persuaded that the safety of the throne was
at stake, she yielded. Next morning Broussel re-
appeared, borne through the streets on men's
shoulders. ' In an hour,' says De Retz, ' the barricades had disappeared, and Paris was as quiet as
if it had been Good Friday.' [1]

With this 27th of August, 1648, the historical
importance of the Fronde really begins and ends.
A civil war followed, and it lasted four years ; but
a very few months of it were sufficient to convince
the Parisian people that from the princes and prin-
cesses, archbishops and rulers, who were professing
to manage and defend their interests, nothing was
to be hoped, and much was to be feared. The

---

[1] De Retz, *Memoirs*, Charpentier's edition, vol. i, pp. 145, 179 ;
De Motteville, vol. ii, pp. 247-275.

wiser councillors of the Parlement were not slow to
see that the bevy of fine ladies and gentlemen who
were actively engaged in parcelling out the rich
provincial governments of France between them, or
creating, when it seemed desirable, fresh sinecures,
were in no respect worthier, and in every way more
expensive, than a strong central government, even
with a Mazarin at its head. Order at any price was
necessary; but the Fronde was disorder at an
extravagantly high price. 'The pleasure of being
waited on by a duke,' says De Motteville, 'may be
very great : *mais les gages de telles gens sont grands* ;
such personages expect very handsome wages for
their services.'[1]

When Louis XVI heard that the Bastille had been
taken, he remarked, ' Why, this is a revolt ! ' ' Sire,'
answered his informant, ' it is not a revolt, it is a
revolution ! ' The insurrection of the Fronde illus-
trates the contrast ; it was not a revolution, but a
revolt. The difference between the insurrection of
the Fronde and the political events, somewhat similar
in appearance, which were going on at the same time
in England, may be summed up in one brief word.
The English Independents had a doctrine, a faith ;
the Frondeurs, even the best of them, had none.
That small minority of brave and noble-hearted men,
who, with the bravest and noblest of all modern
statesmen at their head, wielded for ten years the
destinies of England, had as definite a purpose, as
fixed a theory of life and of government as the band
of heroes who, in the seventh century, fled from
Mecca to Medina with the Arabian prophet. To

[1] De Motteville, vol. ii, p. 502.

carry out their ideal of a Christian polity, and make it a living reality, a practical standard of social life ; to sweep away all social distinctions but those based on spiritual superiority, or, as they would call it, on Divine election ; to recognise no political alliances except those based on the religious principle of encouraging the Protestant interest and suppressing Popery ; such was the Puritan faith, modified, no doubt, in practice by the extraordinary practical wisdom of Cromwell, but acknowledged by his followers, and indeed by its narrowness most seriously hampering the genius of the leader. The English Puritans, I repeat, had a faith ; by virtue of that faith they did mighty things, and by reason of the incompleteness of that faith even their mighty efforts failed, and the Cromwellian revolution,—that one of our revolutions which alone deserves the name of Glorious,—was yet, as far as its avowed purpose went, essentially abortive. Its permanent value consisted in the strong stimulus it gave to free political and religious thought. By it men's minds were educated, the minds of isolated thinkers in England first, and subsequently of a far larger public in France ; for that far greater revolution four generations afterwards, by its more complete destruction of the old, and by the more perfect preparation that in the meantime had been made for social reconstruction, has initiated a new era in the history of Man.

But the insurrectionists of the Fronde had no guiding political principle whatever. Of the utter vacuity, of the self-seeking frivolity of its aristocratic leaders I have said enough. *Non ragioniam di lor.*

But I speak of the bourgeoisie of France ; of that
cultivated professional non - aristocratic class from
which, during the sixteenth, seventeenth, and eighteenth centuries, almost all that makes her illustrious
among the nations has proceeded ;  I speak especially
of her legists, whose influence in the present century
it is perhaps time to diminish rather than increase,
but who, from the thirteenth to the eighteenth century, have played so honourable a part in eliminating
the aristocratic element from France, and in replacing
feudal customs by sounder principles of civil justice.
The legists of France had, from the time of St.
Louis, always supported the monarchical element of
feudalism against the aristocratic.   Guided by the
traditions of the Roman Empire, they felt that in
the strength of the central power lay the surest
guarantee that the forces of the nation would be
concentrated to public and national purposes.   The
time for republicanism not being come, it was far
easier to approximate to the real purpose of republicanism by a strong monarchy than by a strong
nobility.   Accordingly they co-operated invariably,
and in no servile spirit, with the founders of the
French monarchy ;  with Louis IX, Louis XI, and
Henry IV.   Richelieu found them strenuous sup-
porters, and indeed without them would have been
powerless.   Stimulated for a brief moment by the
contagious example of the English revolutionists,
they broke from their traditions.   The English constitutional system tempted them, as French revolutionists have so frequently been tempted, into the
dangerous error of limiting the monarchical power by
checks which, under the decorous veil of popular

self-government, simply substitute for monarchy the far more oppressive influence of oligarchical cliques. It is to the credit of the French Parlements that, after three years' experience of aristocratic misrule, they awoke from their delusion. They abandoned the unprincipled and traitorous intriguers, the Condés, the Bouillons, the Épernons, whose miserable ambition would have parcelled their country into petty principalities, and so degraded her to the political level of Germany. Condé's reckless massacre of unoffending citizens at the Hôtel de Ville, in July, 1652, opened their eyes to their true political position ; they rallied round the monarchy as, for the present, the safeguard of French destinies ; Mazarin, twice banished, was for the second and last time recalled ; and, after four years of civil war, the royal power was firmly fixed at Paris, not to be shaken till, four generations afterwards, the storm came that was finally to uproot it.

In 1659 Mazarin fulfilled the great object of his life, the Treaty of the Pyrenees, which ended the war with Spain. Two years afterwards he died ; and Louis XIV, now twenty-four years old, resolved to govern France with his own hands. The man himself, the outer man at least, is probably better known than any character in history ; and I have no pretension to repeat a portrait which has been drawn so frequently and so elaborately from the life by many a cunning hand. Who is there who cannot picture to himself the dignified courtesy, the gracious, affable address, the chivalrous respect for women of every rank, and all the other virtues of social intercourse between man and man, and between man and

E

woman, which made the French Court the model for
Europe ?    But with the Court of Louis XIV our business does not lie.    The practical results of the man
himself to France and to Europe are what we want
to know.    His blood was strangely mixed, and his
character was mixed not less doubtfully.    Every
feature of it might be traced to his Spanish or to his
French ancestry.    From Anne of Austria came the
sublime and somewhat stolid pride ; the Spanish
dignity intensified by solid Austrian phlegm, the
chill and tardy flow of thought, the proud diffidence
of his powers, and the nervous fear of ridicule and
failure.    From his French grandfather came the
nobler and more generous aspects.    The shrewd
Gascon sense of Henry of Navarre had left its traces.
Something, too, Louis had inherited of his large
views of policy, of the true patriotic instinct ; some
traditional sense of the grandeur of his position ;
the position envied by the great Frederick, the first
position incomparably in the civilized world.    Nor
was he destitute of honest sympathies for the misery
of his fellow - countrymen, nor wanting in noble
ardour to relieve them, so far as his power extended.
The conception of France, happy and prosperous at
home, powerful and respected abroad ; of France as
the centre of the European state-system, more than
a match for any other single state, and fearless even
of combined attacks ; of France, lastly, as the leader
of the movement of thought in Europe, the patroness
of intellect and art in every sphere and in every
nation : this grand conception was not wholly wanting to him.

Under such a ruler, a political bystander, placed

at the middle of the seventeenth century, would not have found it easy to foretell the immediate destinies of France. Two things only were clear. First, the young Louis was determined not to be a puppet-king, a king who, after the fashion invented by the English aristocracy in 1688, was to reign and not to govern. Secondly, that being keenly sensitive to the opinion of those around him, and not being endowed with that innate energy and genius which seizes on an ideal far distant, and relentlessly pushes on to its realization, he would fall unconsciously under the influence of men stronger than himself, who should master the secret springs of his character, make themselves indispensable to him by indefatigable industry and mastery of official detail, and, without his knowing it, suggest the measures that they professed only to execute at his bidding. It would be obvious that on the character and genius of these counsellors would depend a most momentous issue. Should the forces of the French government, concentrated as they now were in a single man, be wielded in a progressive or in a retrograde direction? Whither the world was tending, the great rulers of England and of France were beginning to find out. To Elizabeth and Cromwell, to Henry IV, Sully, and Richelieu, war and foreign conquest were no longer the primary occupation of rulers. War, when they engaged in it, was a necessary evil, accepted only for the sake of peace. They saw, dimly indeed and incompletely, but still they saw, the two grand tendencies of the modern world : peaceful industry in the temporal sphere, and morality based upon unfettered thought in the spiritual. Was Louis XIV to be the successor of these men ?    Or was he to reject the noble tradition of peace and of tolerance, run counter to the current of the world's history, crush, as far as in him lay, the nascent germs of progress, assume the mantle, not of Henry IV, but of Philip of Spain, and allow France to become for a time the retrograde element in Europe?

Of these opposite hypotheses, each in turn proved true. The fifty-four years which elapsed from the death of Mazarin to the death of Louis XIV may be divided into two periods of unequal magnitude. The first period, of eleven years, terminates with the Dutch war of 1672. During this period, Colbert was supreme in the counsels of France. Under his guidance the whole energy of the State was concentrated, as it had never been before, on a pacific development of its commerce, industry, and intellect. These are the years that have given such lustre to the reign of Louis, the only years that can claim honourable mention in history. During the second and far longer period, retrograde influences became gradually supreme. The influence of Louvois, eclipsing that of Colbert, plunged France into a long series of aggressive wars ; the Edict of Nantes was revoked ; the Jesuits worked their will ; and, for the last thirty years of Louis's life, they turned France into a second Spain.

As Mazarin had been bequeathed to France by Richelieu, so Jean Baptiste Colbert was bequeathed by Mazarin. The son of a respectable tradesman of Rheims, he had come to Paris to learn his business and push his fortunes ; had been introduced by an influential relative to Mazarin, who, with a quick eye for financial talent, had taken him into his service as the steward of his enormous establishment. As Mazarin died worth £5,000,000 sterling of our money, gathered together from very questionable sources, the steward had excellent opportunities of probing to their core the monstrous abuses of the French treasury. Fouquet, the Superintendent of Finance, was accumulating plunder with a reckless rapidity only equalled by his lavish expenditure in luxury and license. His establishment was maintained at a yearly cost, it was said, of four millions of francs. His palace at Vaux, far exceeding in splendour the royal palace of Fontainebleau or Saint Cloud, was built at a cost of three-quarters of a million sterling. The leaden pipes that served the fountains of his garden were sold by the Duke de Villars, a hundred years afterwards, for 490,000 francs. His rapacity was a matter of such notoriety, that at his celebrated banquet of August, 1661, when Molière's play, *Les Fâcheux*, was performed before the Court and six thousand guests, the King, irritated at the impudent display of ill-gotten wealth, was on the point of ordering his arrest there and then. Fear of the culprit's power alone deterred him. Fouquet had bought golden opinions everywhere. His possessions on the coast of Brittany were strongly fortified; and papers found in his possession after his arrest, proved what was then suspected, that he was prepared for nothing less than a revival of civil war. Wild as the scheme was, it was enough to frighten the Government to take singular precautions. 'Of all the affairs,' wrote Louis to his son, 'that I have had to manage, this of the arrest of Fouquet has given me the most trouble and anxiety.' He was arrested by stealth, and unawares, at Nantes, and imprisoned at Pignerol till his death in 1680.[1]  Colbert succeeded ; not indeed to the post of superintendent of finance, for Louis had openly declared that for the future he would be his own superintendent and his own prime minister ; but under the humble title of chief clerk of the Council of Finance, Colbert rapidly assumed the substance of both offices, and left his royal master well contented with the shadow.

He found French finance ruined by twenty-five years of war, by the dissensions of the Fronde, and by the peculations of his predecessor.  The gross receipts in the first year of his office, 1661, amounted to 84,000,000 of francs (equal probably to about £8,000,000 at present).  But of this 84,000,000, 52,000,000 were absorbed by interest on loans ; leaving the net revenue only 32,000,000.  In six years he had made such a clearance of the Augean stables, that while the gross receipts had increased 10 per cent, the net revenue had increased 90 per cent ; and at the end of his eleventh year of office, in 1671, the net receipts had increased 140 per cent, while the addition to the year's revenue was only 23.[2]  This astonishing result was obtained by redemption of State loans, and by vigorous prosecu-tion of the financial peculators who, for the last

[1] For a most interesting account of Fouquet's administration, con-spiracy, and trial, see introduction to P. Clément's *Histoire de Colbert* ; a work which contains much valuable and authentic information relative to the financial condition of France during the seventeenth ce itury.

[2] That is to say, the gross revenue was 104,000,000, against 84,000,000 ; the net revenue, 77,000,000 against 32,000,000.

twenty-four years, had played their game with
impunity.   A High Court of Justice was established
to inquire into the books of these gentry ; and
under its firm pressure they disgorged a sum equal to
£16,000,000 sterling of our money.

A brief sketch of what Colbert did, and what he
vainly tried to do, is all that can be here attempted.
It is not too much to say that, had his policy pre-
vailed, the horrors of the French Revolution, and of
the counter-revolution that followed it, would have
been spared.   The French Revolution itself would
none the less have taken place ; nay, it would have
taken place probably far sooner.   But the inevitable
disappearance of the last relics of feudalism, the
inevitable transition from hereditary monarchy to
republican government, from an antiquated State
religion to spontaneous forms of faith better adapted
to the time, would have taken place, not without a
struggle, but without the sanguinary tragedy, without
the military orgies that for twenty years convulsed
and paralysed Europe.   But it was not so to be.

Colbert's schemes of government embraced every
sphere except one.   Reform of judicial abuses,
codification of the law, establishment of an efficient
police, a just system of taxation, freedom to internal
commerce, encouragement to manufactures and to
agriculture, development of the canal system, formation of new colonies, creation of the French navy,
—such was the programme of the last statesman
worthy of the name, if we except the two short
years of Turgot, who was to administer the Government of France till the Revolution.   One department
only he did not dare to touch ; and yet, as a great

minister of finance, if on no other ground, he must
have longed to handle it. The annual revenues of
the established church of France, from tithe and
from landed property, were estimated a hundred
years afterwards at 200,000,000 of francs; equal at
least to £10,000,000 of our money.[1] In the latter
half of the seventeenth century, after the conquests
of Louis XIV in Flanders and elsewhere, they were,
as far as can be ascertained (for ecclesiastical bodies
have always been jealous of accurate estimates of
their income), not much less. It would be perfectly
safe to say that the revenue of the Church was, at
the time of Colbert's ministry, not less than the
revenue of the State. And yet this vast income
was almost wholly exempt from taxation. In the
social system of old France, two of the three estates
of the realm, the nobility and the clergy, paid no
direct taxes. They were exempt from the *taille*
and the *gabelle*, that is, from the property-tax and
the salt-tax, which formed four-fifths of the revenue.

The reason for this exemption is to be sought
far back in the Middle Ages, when feudalism was a
reality, and the spiritual power of Catholicism was
still vigorous and vital. The feudal barons were
supposed to serve their sovereign, and in the best
times of the Middle Ages did really serve him, with
their sword far more than with their purse. But
their right over the soil was not in its origin absolute,
as it afterwards tended to become; and as in England,
whether to the national gain or loss may be questioned,

---

[1] See *Église de France*, by the Abbé Delbos, vol. i, p. 59, quoted in
Louis Blanc's *Hist. de la Révolution Française*, vol. ii, p. 311. The
tithes were estimated at 120,000,000, other property at 80,000,000.

it still remains.   It depended on the will of the
suzerain, and was conditional on the performance of
certain duties, or, subsequently, on the payment of
certain dues.   But on both sides of the Channel feudal
institutions had become degenerate, if not decrepit ;
and the similarity in the process of degeneration is
interesting to notice.   At the restoration of Charles II,
or, as that period may more justly be called, the
accession to supreme power of the English aristocracy,
the question of dealing with these feudal dues was
raised.   If mere justice were to be considered, how
to deal with them was obvious.   The lords of England
held the land of England in consideration of important
services, defence of the soil, defence of the sovereign,
etc., yearly rendered.   The occasion of these particular
services having passed away, they should have been
commuted for an equitable land-tax.   But a Parliament of landowners preferred to raise the required
sum by excise duties ; [1] and the land-tax in England,
in the middle of the nineteenth century (the rental,
by the mere increase of population and industry,
having meantime enormously increased), still remains
at a mere fraction of the sum to which an equitable
system of taxation would raise it.[2]

In France a similar result had been obtained in a
different way.   The old duty of military service had

[1] ' Two schemes (for the commutation of military tenures) were
suggested, the one a permanent tax on lands held in chivalry ; the
other an excise-duty on beer, and some other liquors.   It is evident
that the former was founded on a just principle, while the latter
transferred a particular burden to the community.   But the self-
interest which so unhappily prevails even in representative assemblies
. . . caused the latter to be carried.'—Hallam's *Constitutional
History*, vol. ii, p. 11, 5th edit.

[2] [*I.e.*, in 1866.]

never, as in England, been completely commuted for
pecuniary payments. The feudal militia had been
replaced, towards the close of the fifteenth century,
by standing armies ; and in these armies the French
nobility were still supposed to serve their king
gratuitously, and on this plea were exempt from all
other direct taxation. The result was a monopoly
to their class, the same monopoly which exists at
present in England,[1] of all high military posts and
of the rich perquisites which they involved, and
immunity from all pecuniary contributions to the
necessities of the State.

So much for the exemption of the noblesse. The
exemption of the clergy is still easier to explain.
The poor missionaries of the seventh and eighth
centuries, who devoted a life of rigorous self-denial
to the physical, moral, and spiritual elevation of
Franks, Gauls, and Saxons, were not very hopeful
subjects for the tax-gatherer, and, at a time when
land was the sole source of taxation, naturally paid
no taxes at all. And when the piety or the remorse
of the great landowners had raised a thick growth of
convents, and endowed them with rich field and
pasture, it was still felt that the men who taught the
poor, and saved the starving from starvation, fulfilled
their full measure of obligations to the State. The
result was an enormous aggregate revenue, supplying
in the better times of the Church the purposes of an
education rate and of a poor-rate, but which, in the
sixteenth, seventeenth, and eighteenth centuries,
became more and more corrupt, more and more

[1] [This was written before the abolition of the purchase system in
1871.]

encrusted with sinecures, more and more separated from the intellectual progress of the nation. The Gallican Church, in short, was undergoing the decay which every religious body representing the faith, not of the whole nation, but only of a dominant sect within the nation, and nevertheless supported by a compulsory charge on the rent of land or on the national income, must infallibly undergo. There was a temporary reform in the Gallican Church during the seventeenth century, induced by the pressure of its Protestant rival. Of this more in the concluding Lecture. Enough to say, that such reform was from its nature only temporary. The clergy of France then, like the noblesse, were exempt from all direct taxation. Occasionally they consented to meet in convocation, and vote what they called a gratuitous donation of a few thousand pounds to Government. But their gigantic revenue, a revenue which, as I have stated, was at least equal to the total revenue of the State, was a mine of wealth which Colbert did not dare to penetrate. The time was not yet ripe.

A few words on the old French system of taxation. When I have said that by far the larger portion of the revenue was raised by direct taxation, 'financial reformers,' and indeed, most students of political economy, might expect to find the system of the old French monarchy comparing favourably with our own, in which six-sevenths are still raised by duties on articles the great bulk of which is consumed by the labouring population. That the principle of direct taxation, consistent as it is with the fundamental rule that each person should pay according to his means, is thoroughly just, no thoughtful person could for a moment dispute.   But the manner in which these direct taxes were assessed was so iniquitous, that the worst abuses of Customs and Excise seemed justice when compared with them.   The *taille* was a tax on property.   Of its principal injustice, the exemption of the clergy and noblesse, I have already spoken.   It must be added that large numbers of the middle class, all holders of Government offices, judicial or financial, had also obtained exemption.   In the outlying provinces of Provence, Dauphiné, Languedoc, Burgundy, and Brittany, the *taille* was raised in a comparatively equitable way.   These provinces were in many ways, as I have before remarked, peculiar and distinct from the rest of France.   Their position will be partly understood by comparing it with the independence of Scotland in the seventeenth, or of Ireland in the eighteenth century.   They had their own elective assemblies, which voted supplies to the Government ; they lived to a great extent under their own peculiar laws.   In these provinces, which taken together made up nearly a third of France, the *taille* was levied not on income or personal property, but on land ; *terres nobles*, the land of nobles or clergy, or land which had been theirs formerly, being exempt.   But in the rest of France the *taille* was an income and property-tax ; not land alone, but every other source of income was assessed.   So far, if we leave out of sight the exemption of the governing classes, the principle of taxation was just enough. It was the mode of its application, added to the iniquity of this exemption, which made it so thoroughly oppressive.[1]

The three great administrators of the seventeenth century, Sully, Richelieu, and Colbert, had seen the cruel injustice of a property-tax, from which the principal owners of property were exempt, and had striven to rectify it. They endeavoured in various ways to convert the tax upon the working and trading class into one that should weigh on all classes without distinction. But they strove in vain. The power of the old French monarchy is sometimes thought to have been absolute. But strong as the monarchy was, strong enough to annihilate the aristocracy as a political power, it was not a match for their internal social power. When the time came for taxing the nation equitably, monarchy and aristocracy crumbled down together. The two institutions were too closely bound up together for a just system of taxation to become possible, unless both were united in desiring it. Colbert, in attempting it, and he never relaxed his efforts to bring it about, was the predecessor of the statesmen of the Convention. The miserable crew of fine ladies and gentlemen around him cannot be said to have seen this. They saw nothing ; were incapable of seeing anything ; but they felt it with the low animal instinct of self-preservation. They feared and they hated that heavy, dark, beetle-browed man, working at his desk fourteen hours a day, rigid and exacting to his underlings, to his own son as severe as to the rest, with his deaf ear and his harsh, gruff refusals to all their piteous appeals for comfortable

[1] See note appended to this Lecture.

sinecures ; with his open eye and his honest, hearty recognition of zeal and talent ; with his utter indifference to quarrels of Jesuit and Jansenist, of Catholic or Huguenot ; seeking only for the men, in every sphere and class, in every trade or profession, who could and would help him in his grand design of advancing the peaceful well-being of the French nation.

To those political theorists (I use the word not in the contemptuous sense in which, to the discredit of English culture, the word in this country is apt to be used, since wise theory in every department of human life is to the full as indispensable as wise practice), to the political theorists who believe that governments are a necessary evil, the limits of which it should be our great object to curtail ; that nothing but the bare protection of life and property falls within their province ; that in all other respects they are from their nature hostile to the welfare of mankind, and have invariably impeded its development, I would recommend the careful study of two periods of French history.    The first is the period of Sully's and Henry IV's government, from the treaty of Vervins in 1598 to the King's assassination in 1610. The second is the administration of Colbert, from 1661 to 1672.    I am not pretending that these two administrations are models for the literal imitation of every modern nation.    For if there is one lesson taught impressively and unmistakably to the philosophical student of history, it is this, that the political institutions of a state are to be judged of not absolutely, but relatively to the degree of intellectual, moral, and social development which

that state may have reached.   The form of government, and the limits of state intervention suited to
one period of its history, may be utterly unsuited to
another.   The continuous problem of re-adapting
the governmental institutions of a country to the
changing phases of its moral and social growth, is
thus one of continuous difficulty ; it is a problem
making constant demands on all the theoretical and
practical wisdom which the nation may have at its
disposal.   But with all the modifications which this
principle of relativity involves, the spirit which
actuated the Governments of Sully and of Colbert
remains immortally admirable.

What they did for the material well-being of
France may be classed under three heads : initiation
of new industries ; liberation of trade from restric-
tions ; creation of new means of transit.

It is constantly repeated in this country, that
no Government has ever at any time succeeded in
implanting permanently any branch of industry in a
country.   When the intervention of Government is
withdrawn, it is said, the manufacture in question
has invariably perished.   Yet no one can deny that
if there is any branch of industry in France which
has at present an intrinsic and independent vitality,
it is the silk manufacture.   It forms by far the
largest item in her exports.   In 1863, France
exported silk, raw and manufactured, to the amount
of £18,000,000.   Now, as an historical fact, it is
certain that the silk-manufacture of France, which
originated in the first instance with Louis XI, was first
developed into its large proportions by Henry IV,
with the help of two men, Olivier de Serres and

Laffemas, whom he called to his counsels. Mulberry trees were planted in the gardens of the Tuileries, and were distributed largely by the Government to the inhabitants of the districts of Paris, Orléans, Tours, and Lyons. The church lands were called into requisition ; and all the bishops and abbots in France were required to devote a certain quantity of their domains for the purpose. Seed was purchased in large quantities, and distributed freely to those who were thought likely to use it. Two or three model establishments were set up by the Government, and placed under the care of artisans brought from Italy. All these measures, at which a certain school of political economists would of course shudder, resulted in the self-supporting silk trade which is now the chief industry of modern France. France, at the beginning of Henry IV's reign, imported silk-stuffs to the amount of £2,500,000 ; the home manufacture being quite inappreciable. A few years after his death, in 1620, France not only supplied her own consumption, but *exported* to Germany, Portugal, and England, to the amount of £5,000,000 sterling. I have not time to notice, even if this were the place to do so, the other features of Henry's industrial administration : his colonies to America ; his treaties of commerce with England, the Hanse towns, Spain, and Turkey,—treaties of which the tariff was not less liberal than those that have been made in late years ; the development of the transit system of the country, both by land and by water. The splendid canal system which France now possesses was initiated in his reign, and under the special en- couragement of Sully ; and the Canal of Briare deserves particular mention, as the first canal in the world which was carried over a watershed. Finally, it should be mentioned that, so far from loading France with debt by these measures, he lightened the taxation by 20 per cent, and yet left in the treasury a surplus equal to one year's income, which was, however, speedily dissipated under the impotent Government which filled up the interval between Sully and Richelieu.

The Thirty Years' War, the Protestant Rebellion, and a continual series of aristocratic conspiracies, left Richelieu little power to develop the industrial progress inaugurated by Sully and Henry IV. But, as his *Political Testament* shows, it was not for want of will. Great efforts were made to diminish the taxes which pressed on the peasant ; the road system and canal system were carried a stage further ; and the intellectual progress of the country was stimulated by the foundation of the French Academy. Mazarin, with his Fronde rebellion, could do little in this direction ; but Colbert found in it free scope for his vast energies.

Colbert has been spoken of by modern writers as if he were the inventor of the theory of protection. Yet, in one sense, and in a very important sense, he was a most vigorous free-trader. France, when he assumed power, was, commercially speaking, not one country, but a federation of states, like modern Germany. Each of its twenty provinces had its own system of customs-duties, which made it practically impossible to transport goods of any bulk from one part of the kingdom to another. This remnant of the old feudal system Colbert set himself to destroy.

F

He endeavoured to make France one country commercially, as Richelieu had made her one politically. Popular prejudice was too strong for perfect success. Three-fourths of the kingdom agreed to his reforms ; but the remaining fourth, including Languedoc, Brittany, Guienne, and Dauphiné still remained separate, as far as customs-duties were concerned, until the Revolution.

A volume would be required to do full justice to his administration ; to his attempted codification of the civil law ; to his organization of the State forests ; to his commercial trading companies for the East Indies, the Mediterranean, and Northern Europe ; to his encouragement of the French cloth manufacture ; and to his marvellous creation of the French navy. He found that navy, in 1661, consisting of thirty small ships ; in 1671 France possessed 190 vessels, of which 120 were ships of the line. Inconsistent as this may seem with the pacific character of his ministry, such a fleet was, I believe, necessary for a country that wished to preserve her commerce and her colonies from the unscrupulous aggression, and from the open connivance at piracy which from the time of Elizabeth had stained English commercial policy.[1] There are features of Colbert's government which admit of less defence. His attempts to cheapen food and to promote industry, by forbidding the exportation of corn, were doubtless futile and suicidal. His minute regulations of the trade-guilds were oppressive and

[1] See Professor Beesly's Essay on 'England and the Sea,' contained in *International Policy ; or Essays on the Foreign Relations of England*.

unwise.   But Colbert is hardly to be held responsible
for these measures.   What he did had been done
repeatedly before, and formed in fact part of the
traditional system of mediæval industry.   If he is
to be blamed, it is only for being not more clear-
sighted in this respect than his predecessors, or than
contemporary statesmen in other countries.   It
must not be forgotten that the last two years of his
administration were years of war, involving desperate
expedients for urgent necessities.   Still the fact
remains, that in his Corn-laws, and in his attempts
to reorganize the industrial guilds of the Middle
Ages, he went far astray.   His zeal for the industrial
welfare of the country was most honourable, and the
errors which misdirected it were shared by the great
mass of his countrymen, until the great English and
French economists of the eighteenth century proved
their fallacy.

We must not forget that his protective system
was based on the principle that a nation should if
possible be, as far as the necessaries of life were
concerned, self-sufficing.   It must also be remembered
that the first great step in that direction had been
taken by England some years before, when Cromwell,
in 1652, passed the Navigation Laws ; laws which
Adam Smith declares to have been, relatively to
that time, of the greatest value.   These laws, and
those of Colbert, were not based on any delusion
that the wealth of the country was increased by
them, but on the necessity of rendering the country
independent in case of attack.   Free trade is possible
in the nineteenth century, because the general framework of European society has become less and less

military, more and more pacific and industrial.   In
the seventeenth century there were still two great
sources of war ever ready to flow: religious animosity
and colonial conquest; and it would have been
madness for any statesman to ignore their existence.
To consider the question of free trade apart from
the general evolution of society, is an error eminently
characteristic of many writers of the day who assume
the title of political economists, although the great
economic writers of the eighteenth century were for
the most part free from it.

The great industrial enterprise of Colbert's age,
the canal which joined the Atlantic to the Mediterranean,—a canal with 75 locks, 162 miles long,
carried over a watershed 830 feet above the sea
level,—deserves special notice.   It was a century
and a half since the great architect, painter, and
engineer, Leonardo da Vinci, had for the first time
practically applied the invention of locks to a canal
in the Lombard plains.   But the credit of first
carrying canals over a watershed, by means of a
system of reservoirs, belongs to a French engineer
of the sixteenth century, Adam de Craponne.   His
principle was first put in practice, as I have mentioned, in the canal of Briare, which connects the
Loire and Seine.   To Riquet belongs the honour of
the magnificent canal of Languedoc, which joined
the Atlantic with the Mediterranean by the rivers
Garonne and Aude.   To this great work Colbert
devoted 7,000,000 francs, the rest being furnished
by the province of Languedoc.

The extent of his encouragement to arts, manufactures, and letters, during the reign of Louis XIV,

is worth stating.   £50,000 were given to the Paris
observatories, £288,000 to the Gobelin and other
Paris manufactures, £136,000 to manufactures in
other parts of France ; finally, £160,000 in pensions
to men of letters.   Considering the large expenditure,
amounting to at least £12,000,000, in unnecessary
royal palaces, and the infinitely larger sum, amounting
probably to not less than £200,000,000, squandered
in foolish and profligate wars, expenditure for which
Louis XIV and Louvois are responsible, the encouragement given by Colbert to intellectual progress
is but a small gnat for the modern economist to
strain at.   The list of pensioners is worth reading.
It contains the names of Pierre Corneille and his
brother, of Molière, Racine, Perrault, the historian
Mézeray, and what is even more remarkable, of many
eminent foreigners ; among them, Vossius the
geographer, and the great Dutch mathematician
Huygens.   The ' Académie française ' had been
formed thirty years before by Richelieu.   Colbert
added the Academy of Inscriptions, the Academy
of Sciences, and the Academy of Painting and
Sculpture ; institutions which, it may be, have now
served their time, and by degenerating into narrow
cliques impede the progress of thought more than
they promote it ; but which, in an age of less
advanced culture, brought the small minority of
educated and thoughtful men into mutual contact,
and aided in making Paris what it has ever since,
with the exception of two short intervals, continued
to be, the centre of European culture.

Such was the administration of Colbert ; the last
of a series of great statesmen who had governed

France for nearly a century. He died in 1683, worn out with toil, and saddened by the failure of his highest hopes. Some time before his death the tide of feudal and Catholic reaction had set in. Aggressive wars had begun, and the revocation of the Edict of Nantes was impending. Within thirty years the spectre of national bankruptcy, which had haunted Colbert's dreams, was to become a flesh-and-blood reality. France would lie prostrate, paralysed, and disgraced, with a national debt of £100,000,000. Ninety shameful years were to pass by before a statesman worthy of Colbert should be called for a brief moment to power. But Turgot found the process of putrefaction too far gone; and after Turgot came the deluge.

### Note on French Theories of Taxation in the Seventeenth Century (p. 61)

We are too apt to fancy that rational notions of taxation and of other economic subjects were unknown in Europe till the publication of Adam Smith's treatise. The history of speculation on these subjects would be interesting, and has not yet been written. The subjoined note relates to two remarkable French writers, little known in this country, whose theories of taxation were such as, even in the present day, we may study with advantage.

The first of these is Pierre le Pesant, sieur de Boisguillebert, a magistrate of Rouen. In his two most important works, *Détail de la France*, and

*Factum de la France*,[1] he lays down the principles of taxation, and discusses their application to the present state of France. He begins by refuting the fallacy that the wealth of a nation consists in its specie. On this point Adam Smith himself is not more eloquent. Gold is not wealth, he remarks. A country may be extremely rich without possessing a grain of the precious metals. The richer, in fact, a country is, the more able is it to dispense with gold and silver. In a state of advanced wealth, a paper currency would suffice. ' La richesse n'est autre chose que le pouvoir de se procurer l'entretien commode de la vie.' ' Tout le fondement et la cause de toutes les richesses de l'Europe sont le blé, le vin, le sel, la toile ; on ne se procure les autres choses qu'à proportion qu'on a plus qu'il ne faut de ceux-ci.' Now, these products, he says, abound in France ; and France, if properly administered, should be the richest country in Europe. Yet the fact is, he continues, that, judging by the simplest test, that is by the amount of consumption of the necessaries of life, the well-being of France is far from being what it was a hundred years before ; from what it is actually in England, notwithstanding her costly wars ; from what it is in those parts of France (the *pays d'états*) where more enlightened principles of taxation prevail.

In taxation the great principle is to do the least possible injury ' à ces deux mamelles de toute la

---

[1] The first of these works was published in 1697 ; the second a few years later. They are reprinted in Daire's collection of *Économistes du dix-huitième siècle.*

république, l'agriculture et la commerce.' But the
actual system of taxation he shows to be equally
ruinous to both.    The two sources of the French
revenue were the excise and customs, and the
property-tax ; the *douanes* and the *taille.*    The
first of these were, by the mode of their administration, fatal to commerce ; the second, equally fatal to
agriculture.    The *taille*, in certain privileged districts
of France (the *pays d'états*, Brittany, Guienne, Languedoc, Provence, Burgundy, etc.) was a land tax ;
and, as far as it went, was levied equitably, leaving
out of sight the preposterous injustice of the exemption of *terres nobles* ; *i.e.*, of land which belonged,
or had originally belonged, to the nobility.    But in
the greater part of France the *taille* was not a land
tax, but a personal tax.    A computation was made
of how much each man was worth, and he was taxed
accordingly.    To the principle itself there was nothing
to object.    We should ourselves do well to make use
of it in the present day.    It was the mode of its
application that was so intolerably oppressive.    The
Privy Council fixed the amount that was to come
from each province.    It was then for the Intendant
of the province to fix the contribution of each parish.
The great object of the parish was of course to make
interest through its seigneur with the Intendant, so
as to be assessed lightly.    Then came the business
of individual assessment.    This was done by the
parishioners for themselves.    For it must be noted
that the French peasant in his worst periods of
physical misery, and these have been frequent and
terrible, has never sunk into the condition of political
degradation and nullity peculiar to agricultural

labourers in England.    Never has the soil of France
been monopolized, as in England, by thirty or forty
thousand persons.    Large numbers of the French
peasantry possessed land long previous to the Revolution ; and still larger numbers were cottiers on the
Irish system.    Moreover, they possessed what the
English labourer has never known, the institution
of village assemblies for purposes of local government.    The villagers met together annually in the
churchyard on a Sunday, after morning service, and
elected seven of their fellow-parishioners to assess the
sum demanded.    Here began a scene of the most
profound disorder.    The members of the committee
often, Boisguillebert assures us, sell their votes to the
wealthier inhabitants of the parish, *i.e.*, promise for a
consideration to do all in their power to exempt them.
All falls on the poorest class.    Often the committee
cannot agree ;  they meet at the wine-shop, and go on
debating the matter there for months.    Meanwhile
the officers of the Intendant are pressing them, holding them solely responsible, and threatening them
with distraint and imprisonment.    He draws a
piteous and ludicrous picture of the committee of
assessors, seven in number, walking down one side
of the street, while the committee of the past year
were collecting their arrears on the other side, often
carrying away pots and pans where no money was
to be had, and pursued from house to house with
curses and imprecations.    Altogether, these assessors
had a bad time of it.    The lawsuits, the quarrellings
and heartburnings created by the system, were in-
credible.    The one inevitable result was to induce
every one to secrete his wealth in odd holes and

corners, to wear as poor clothing and live as scantily as possible, so as not to appear rich. Adding the tolls demanded by the seigneur of each village, his monopoly of the corn-mill, of the wine-press, and of the bridge ; adding the Government monopoly of salt, and the compulsory distribution of certain quantities of it to each individual at a fixed price ; adding the cumbrous and vexatious system of Excise which, from the expense of its collection, and above all, by the discouragement it gave to trade, took from the people, as Boisguillebert remarks, ten times the amount that it brought into the treasury ; we get some slight conception of the miseries of French taxation in the seventeenth and eighteenth centuries.

In an imaginary dialogue which he supposes to take place between the king and a Normandy farmer who is bargaining with him for the lease of Crown lands, he puts the matter clearly and amusingly enough. The king, in the most candid manner, is explaining to the farmer the conditions to which his life there will be subject : ' When you wish to purchase a cask of wine, you will have to pay seventeen dues at seven or eight different offices, which are only open at certain hours of certain days. If you fail in any one of them, whatever delay it may cost you, the wine and the carriage which conveys it will all be confiscated for the benefit of the officials. And I may observe that their word in the matter will always be taken against yours. Again, when you want to sell your goods at a reasonable price, I shall put such a heavy tax upon them that your customers will prefer buying them elsewhere. I shall derive little good from all this, and you will lose the whole

value of your labour ; but such is our system.    Often
you will find it impossible to sell your liquors, though
a day's journey off they may be selling at an extravagant price.    But if you should be induced by this
price to take your goods there, you will probably find
it of little use, for there are various tolls on the way
which I have farmed out, the formalities of which
are extremely difficult to observe.    The loss to you
in this is ten times as great as the gain to me, but I
am told that it is for my advantage to have things
managed thus.    Besides this, you will have to pay
me yearly a sum bearing no fixed relation to your
property, varying indeed from one parish to another,
so that it will be most desirable for you to curry
favour with the officials who assess this tax.    I
should advise you not to be too regular about the
payment of your taxes.    The assessors find it
thoroughly answers to engage in a good deal of liti-
gation.    And indeed, if I found that they gathered
in their taxes too easily, I should certainly not farm
the taxes to them on such favourable terms.    It will
be desirable for you to live as meanly and poorly as
possible, or you will assuredly be assessed at a higher
rate.    Hide up your savings in any odd corner ;
beware of investing them.    Avoid for the same
reason putting any beasts on your land to manure
it. . . . I may mention, also, that the business of
collection, which is extremely onerous, will fall on
you every three or four years ; the tax-farmer will
hold you responsible for the amount, and will dis-
train and imprison you if it is not forthcoming.'

To which the farmer replies : 'Sire, I presume
that all you wish is to receive a certain amount

of money. Now, the plan you have been describing seems expressly invented for the purpose of ruining yourself and me at the same time. Your wealth and mine can only come from the sale of the produce of our land, and this plan makes it impossible or difficult to grow any produce. Now, I offer to pay your Majesty exactly double the sum you ask for, provided only that you will allow me to consume what I please, to grow what I please, and to sell where and how I please. The bargain will be an excellent one for me, for I shall make ten times my present profits.'[1]

'The interests of the Government and the people,' Boisguillebert continues, 'rightly understood, are precisely identical; yet the Government spoliates the people like a hostile country, by quartering on them armies of tax-gatherers, and laying the whole burden of taxation on that part of the population which is least able to bear it. And, in the end, the upper classes suffer by this plan as much as the lower. You have a given cargo to carry from Paris to Lyons with forty horses; you put the whole weight on three of them; when these are knocked up you try three more, and so on till you have killed the whole.' The burden was not too much for the forty, but by unequal division the whole are ruined by it. 'Il en va de la pauvreté,' he remarks in an admirable illustration, 'comme des diamants; il y a de certains degrés où tout nouveau surcroît double et triple son effet, tant pour celui qui les souffre que pour l'État.' Take from a poor cottier the twelve pounds with which he had been intending to buy manure for his land, the loss to the State is incalculable; perhaps as

---

[1] *Détail de la France*, Daire's edition, pp. 236-238.

much as £200, for the land goes out of cultivation in consequence.   Whereas the same sum taken from a rich man would produce comparatively slight injury.

The remedies proposed by Boisguillebert were equitable distribution of the property tax, abolition of Excise, and reduction of import duties.   His book created considerable excitement, and had the honour of being suppressed.   It gave rise to another work of still greater consequence, the *Dîme Royale* of Marshal Vauban ; [1] one of the noblest and strongest characters in the seventeenth century.   As a military engineer, he had travelled and resided in every province of France, and had thought deeply on the financial chaos and physical misery that surrounded him.  He finds, after careful inquiry during many years, that there are in France a tenth of the population who are beggars ;  five-tenths on the verge of beggary ; three-tenths deeply involved in debt.   ' In the remaining tenth,' he says, ' I include the clergy, the noblesse, the legal profession, government officials, and the higher mercantile class.   Of these there may be some hundred thousand families ; and I think I am not wrong when I say that there are not more than ten thousand of these who can be described as comfortably off.'

The most obvious remedy for this state of things was equitable taxation ; abolition, above all, of the iniquitous exemption from taxation of precisely the classes best able to bear it.   One plan would be to substitute the *taille réelle* for the *taille personnelle* throughout France ; in other words, to collect the revenue by a land-tax.   The objection to this, he says, is the difficulty of framing anything like an

---

[1] Also published in Daire's collection.

equitable valuation of the land, owing to the constant alterations which are occurring in its value.
Besides, there are certain lands called *terres nobles*
(although not necessarily occupied by noblemen),
which are exempted; distinctions which ought not
to exist, but which are difficult to abolish. The
simplest and most equitable method of taxation, in
his opinion, is that of which we have an example in
the Church Tithe. He asserts that of all taxes,
there is none which is collected with so little difficulty or disturbance. The machinery for collecting
it already exists, and might with great ease be
extended to the collection of a State tithe. This
he would fix somewhere between a twentieth and
a tenth. The former, that is to say, a 5 per cent
tax upon the yearly produce of the land, would bring
in about 60,000,000 of livres. He arrives at this by
a careful examination of the returns of Church tithe.

This is the first of the four items of which his
scheme of taxation consists. The second is a tax
of 5 per cent levied on all income not coming
under the previous head, estimated as follows :—

|  | Livres. |
|---|---|
| House-tax . . . . . . | 1,600,000 |
| Mills . . . . . . . | 742,000 |
| Shipping . . . . . . | 300,000 |
| Interest of funded property . . . | 1,000,000 |
| Government salaries, pensions, etc. . . | 2,000,000 |
| Judicial fees . . . . . . | 500,000 |
| Commercial incomes . . . . | 2,000,000 |
| Servants' wages . . . . . | 1,500,000 |
| Artisans, journeymen, assessed at $3\frac{1}{3}$ per cent instead of 5 per cent . . . | 6,000,000 |
| Total . . . | 15,642,000 |

His third item is the salt-tax. In place of the foolish and iniquitous system of compelling people to buy a fixed quantity of salt from Government officials, and forbidding them to buy it elsewhere, he proposes that the State shall buy up the salt-marshes, and sell the produce freely to all buyers at a moderate profit. From this source he computed a revenue of 23,400,000 livres.[1]

Finally, Vauban proposed to raise, under the head of customs, stamp duties, and assessed taxes, 18,000,000 livres. Those who compare the proportion which in Vauban's system direct taxation bore to indirect, with that which it bears in England at the present day, will judge how far he was in advance of his time. He was well aware of the opposition which his book would meet with. ' It will be opposed,' he said, ' by all finance-officers, farmers-general, tax-gatherers, the higher clergy, the nobility, lawyers, all who have obtained exemption under any pretext whatever,'—' enfin tous ceux qui savent pêcher en eau trouble, et s'accommoder au dessus du roi et du public, n'approuveront point un système qui doit couper par la racine toutes les pilleries qui s'exercent dans la levée des revenus de l'État.' He was not mistaken ; his book, published in 1707, aroused a storm of indignation, and its circulation was prohibited. It savoured far too strongly

---

[1] The monstrous abuses of the *gabelle* continued unaltered, with so many others, till the French Revolution. In 1781 the revenue from salt was 72,000,000 livres ; the cost of collection being 18,000,000. There were, on an average, 3,500 convictions annually for smuggling. In 1782 an edict was launched against those who kept a peculiar breed of large dogs specially trained to carry contraband salt from Anjou to Brittany.

of the Revolution.   The popular sympathies expressed in it are remarkable.   ' It seems to me,' he
says, ' that sufficient account has never been taken
in France of the lower class of the population, and
that, in consequence, it is the most miserable of any
in the kingdom.   And yet it is the most important
of all classes, whether you look at its numbers, or at
the actual services which it renders.   It is the
working-class who bear the whole burden of taxation ;
who have always endured, and are now enduring,
more than any other. . . . It is the lower orders of
the people who, by their labour and trade, and by
their contributions to taxation, enrich the king and
his kingdom ; it is they who fill the ranks of our
armies and navies ; to whom we owe all our retail
trade, all our manufactures ; who supply us with
labourers for our vineyards and corn-lands ; in
fact, it is this class who do all the productive work,
whether in town or country. . . . The more money
you draw from the people by taxation, the less you
have to spend in trade ; and there is no money in
the kingdom so well employed as that which is left
in their hands.   There, you may be sure, it is
never lying idle or useless.' [1]

These remarks are worthy of one of the noblest
of warriors, of the man by whom war was always
regarded as the instrument of peace ; who even
in war was always parsimonious of bloodshed.
' J'aimerais mieux,' he said to Louis XIV at the siege
of Cambrai in 1672, ' avoir conservé cent soldats à
votre Majesté que d'en avoir ôté trois mille à
l'ennemi.'    'Il vaut mieux,' he said on another

[1] *Dîme Royale*, Daire's ed., pp. 44-47.

occasion, 'verser moins de sang, dût-on brûler un peu plus de poudre.' In 1703, he offered to accompany La Feuillade to the siege of Turin as his subordinate. 'What!' said the King, 'you a marshal, and he only a lieutenant-general?' 'Sire,' he answered, 'ma dignité est de servir l'État: je laisserai le bâton de maréchal à la porte, et j'aiderai peut-être M. de la Feuillade à entrer dans la ville.'

He died in 1707, shortly after the publication of his views on taxation, the contemptuous rejection of which must have saddened his last hours. He had conducted fifty-three sieges, had built thirty-three fortresses, and repaired three hundred.

G

# LECTURE III

IN the middle of the seventeenth century, a treaty
was made at Münster, in Westphalia, to which most
of the States of Western Europe were parties, and
which marks one of the great eras in history. It
put an end to the war which for thirty years had
desolated Germany ; it established irrevocably the
fact that the Christian world was for the future to
consist of two rival sections, all hope of preponderance for either being utterly cut off ; and it laid
the foundation of the present constitution of the
European Commonwealth. Between the period that
elapsed from the Treaty of Westphalia in 1648 to
the death of Louis XIV in 1715, five European
treaties were made : that of the Pyrenees in 1659,
of Aix-la-Chapelle in 1668, of Nimeguen in 1678,
of Ryswick in 1697, and of Utrecht in 1713. But
those who for the first time examine the alterations
which these treaties made in the map of Europe,
and who bear in mind that forty years out of the
sixty-five were years of European war, are astonished
to see how slight are the territorial changes, and
look back with admiration at the singular stability

82

of the political equilibrium, the Balance of Power, established in 1648 by the genius of modern diplomacy.

Fully to appreciate the historical importance of an event so big with consequences for the European future, it is necessary for a moment to throw a somewhat far-reaching glance into the European past.  Nor is any apology needed for this ; since the value of history depends almost entirely upon our power of regarding it as a continuous and connected whole.  Needful as it may be for our feeble powers of comprehension to dwell for a moment on an isolated portion of the picture, to listen exclusively to a single movement of the symphony, to study the functions of a special portion of the organism, we must never forget that the history of Western Europe from the Roman Republic to the French Revolution, is a continuous and unbroken series, the general law of which can only be grasped by comparing the successive links.

Of the five populations that make up the Western State-system, the Italian, Spanish, French, British, and German, the first four were incorporated into the Roman Empire.  In the ninth century, Charlemagne completed the work which the Romans had not been able to accomplish.  By advancing the frontiers of civilization from the Rhine to the Elbe, he forestalled the last danger of barbarian invasion ; and Germany now took her place as an integral member of the Western Republic.  His celebrated revival of the Western Empire had its temporary value.  Unreal and fictitious as the name of Empire was even then, the prestige which it bore served as a

rallying point until the real bond of union between
Western nations, the spiritual power of the Catholic
Church, was fully established.    For it cannot be too
often repeated, that the principal contrast between
Mediæval Europe and the Europe of the Roman
Empire lay in the fact that the latter was bound
together by the compulsory force of military government, or, when the necessity for war had ceased, by
a uniform administrative system ; the Europe of the
Middle Ages by the moral force of a common faith
and a common spiritual authority.

But the treaty of Verdun in 843 was really the
recognition that France, Germany, and Italy were
for the future to have a separate existence.    Spain
and Britain had never been included even by
Charlemagne.    Mediæval Europe was a loose and
shifting collection of innumerable feudal States,
falling more and more distinctly every century into
one of the five populations which I have mentioned ;
owning more and more definitely a central authority,
either German, Spanish, British, or French, to which
allegiance was to be paid, but held together by the
far stronger tie of membership in the Catholic Church,
and subordination to the Papal authority.    The
political action of this aggregate of States upon the
world outside it, differed widely from that of the
Roman Empire.    For ancient Rome, the one ab-
sorbing object was aggressive war ; the conquest of
the surrounding nations, and their incorporation into
her own system of polity.    It is her glory that she
accomplished this work ;    and that war, the sole
honourable employment for free men in the ancient
world, became in her hands, what it had seldom

been before, the instrument of human progress, the high road of modern civilization.   But for Mediæval Europe, war, which still remained as the most honourable, if not the only honourable occupation for the governing class, had changed its purpose. From being aggressive, it had become defensive. The object was no longer to incorporate fresh nations by conquest into Western civilization, but to protect that civilization against the aggressions of the Pagan and Mohammedan world.   The campaigns of Charles Martel against the Arab invaders of Spain and Southern France, in the eighth century, and those of Charlemagne in the next generation against the Saxons, obviously defended Christian civilization from the most imminent peril.   Not less necessary for the same purpose were the Crusades of the eleventh, twelfth, and thirteenth centuries.   If we remember the terror caused by the Mongol invasions in the thirteenth and fourteenth centuries, and that at the very end of the seventeenth century Austria saw the Ottoman beneath the walls of her capital, we shall be more ready to believe that the Popes, in stimulating Western Europe to the Crusades, were guided not by mad fanaticism, but by wise and statesmanlike instincts.

In this defensive system of European warfare, one of the five populations I have mentioned had stood out with peculiar prominence.   France, which under the Carlovingian dynasty had been the scene of the great series of battles which turned the tide of Mohammedan invasion, was in the twelfth and thirteenth centuries the mainspring of the crusading movement.   The first Crusade was preached in

Central France by Peter of Amiens, and was headed
by Robert of Normandy, by Godfrey of Bouillon, by
Hugo, brother of Louis, and by Raymond of Toulouse ; the second was inspired by the preaching of
Bernard of Clairvaux ; in the third, Philip of France
shared the work with Frederick of Germany and
Richard of England ; the fourth was principally
headed by French noblemen ; and the sixth (for
the fifth was merely nominal) was entirely conducted
by St. Louis.    The action of France in the Crusades
is the first of her titles to political precedence in
Europe.[1]

The beginning of the fourteenth century, two
centuries before the insurrection of Martin Luther,

[1] The scene of Ariosto's great poem, representing the struggle of
the East and West, ranges occasionally over every part of Europe
and of Asia.    But for the most part it lies in France, and the central action of the poem, to which all the rest gravitates, is at Paris.
The greatest of the Orders of Chivalry was founded entirely by
Frenchmen ; and at the time of its suppression they constituted a
large majority.    In the Order of Hospitallers, the second in importance, Frenchmen preponderated no less.    Intellectually, the claims of
France to precedence during the Middle Ages may be questioned by
the Tuscans, but by no one else.    The University of Paris was the
centre of the great philosophical movements of the time.    The central position of France in Western Europe has of course favoured,
as it still favours, her influence.    Another cause is to be sought in
the fact, that she, of all the western nations, if Italy be left out,
has the most continuous history.    Italy has had continuity, but continuity without unity.    English history dates from the consolidation
of the Saxon power.    German history begins with the treaty of
Verdun ; the continuity of Spanish development was broken by the
Saracen conquest.    But the history of the French people begins with
the Roman conquest.    The invasion of the Franks and other Teu-
tonic tribes was a very important modifying influence, as was our
Norman invasion, or that of the Tartars in China ; but the Franks
did not, like the Saxons in Britain, cut short the national filiation
and begin afresh ; although this has been imagined the case by those
to whom the history of a nation consists in the annals of its
dynasties.

may be fixed upon as the period when the disruption
of the Catholic system became evident and certain.
Into the causes of that disruption we have not now
to enter.    Enough to say, that the miserable anarchy
of the fourteenth and fifteenth centuries, of which
the purposeless invasion of France by the English
was but one though the most striking example, was
the first result of the absence of a central mediating
power which kings and emperors had been forced to
respect.    The old basis of order was shifting under
men's feet, and the materials for the new order,
based on free scientific inquiry, and peaceful and
unfettered industry, were as yet very few and scanty
except in Italy.    It is to the eternal credit of
Louis XI that, at the end of the fifteenth century, he
should so clearly have grasped this conception of
industrial as opposed to military government.

In the sixteenth century, the open rupture of the
religious world into two opposing and irreconcilable
sects threatened the State system of Europe with a
new danger.    Protestantism, with the revolutionary
outgrowths which accompanied its very first appearance, and which seemed indeed inseparable from its
nature, was an object of terror to Conservative
statesmen ; and not less formidable were the untenable claims of the retrograde party to reassert the
old supremacy of their faith by whatever means and
at whatever cost.    And the religious wars which
convulsed France and other countries during the
sixteenth century were still further complicated by
the pretensions of the Austrian power to universal
empire.    Charles V, inheriting Spain, the two Sicilies,
and the American colonies from Ferdinand of Aragon

and from Isabella of Castile ; Holland, Belgium, and
Franche Comté from Mary of Burgundy ; and the
hereditary provinces of Austria from Maximilian,
concentrated in himself a territorial power unknown
since the days of Charlemagne.    And when in 1520
he added to these vast forces the still illustrious
title of Emperor, the shadow cast over Europe was
ominous and threatening.    France resisted his preponderance in vain, and to her cost.    And when
Philip II succeeded to most of the substantial portion
of his father's power, added Portugal to Spain, and
openly avowed his crusade against the heretics of
England and of Holland, the danger to civilization
reached its acme.    The glorious revolt of the Dutch
Provinces in 1572 was the first step to meet that
danger ; the defeat of the Spanish Armada in 1588
was the second ; and the third was the accession of
Henry of Navarre to the French throne, and the
compromise of Protestant with Catholic, known as
the Edict of Nantes (1598).

Such were the conditions that forced upon the
minds of the wiser European statesmen the necessity
of common action in the cause of European welfare.
The 'Great Design,' for great, immortally great, it
surely was, of Henry of France, aided, as Sully tells
us, by Elizabeth of England, is the first indication of
an Occidental, as opposed to a purely national, policy,
which had been seen since the days of the Crusades.
Utopian in detail, but profoundly true in principle,
the scheme of Henry IV boldly put forward the
conceptions, so startling for that age, of Western
Europe as a peaceful confederacy of free states ;
of a common council to arbitrate in international

disputes ; of mutual toleration for the three recognised sects—Catholic, Lutheran, and Calvinist ;
and thus of the removal of any future cause for
European war. It is particularly to be noted that
the map of Europe, as he planned it, included not
the slightest augmentation of French territory. ‘His
intention,’ says Sully, his prime minister and intimate
friend, ‘ was voluntarily and for ever to relinquish all
power of augmenting his dominions ; not only by
conquest, but by all other just and lawful means.
By this he would have discovered the secret to
convince all his neighbours that his whole design
was to save both himself and them those immense
sums which the maintenance of so many thousand
soldiers, so many fortified places, and so many
military expenses require ; to free them for ever
from the fear of those bloody catastrophes so
common in Europe ; to procure them an uninterrupted
repose ; and, finally, to unite them all in an in-
dissoluble bond of security and friendship.’ [1]

[1] *Memoirs*, b. xxx, p. 332. Eng. trans., 4to, 1761. [This
passage needs considerable modification in the light of recent investigation. M. Mariéjol, in vol. vi of Lavisse's *Histoire de France*, compares
the ideas attributed to Henry IV with the King's actual policy, and
points out how practical are his acts and how widely they contrast in
character, aim, and method, with the plans attributed to him by Sully.
He declares the ‘ Great Design ’ to be mainly an Utopia, born of the
struggles of the Reformation period. ‘À toutes ces utopies Sully
ajouta les visions que lui suggéra dans sa longue vieillesse le dépit de
son impuissance. Depuis la mort du Roi son maître, il vécut dans la
disgrâce. Il vit le commencement, le milieu et put prévoir la fin de
la carrière de Richelieu ; il assista, oisif et inutile, au succès d'une
politique dirigée contre la maison d'Autriche. Il dut se dire alors et
il finit par croire qu'Henri IV, s'il avait vécu, aurait aussi bien fait
sinon mieux. Et il mit tous ses soins et nul scrupule à le persuader à
la postérité.’ It may be added that the English translation from
which Dr. Bridges quotes is by no means a close rendering of Sully's
*Œconomies royales.*]

Of the many steps that lay between this great statesman and his noble ideal, one at least was immediate and obvious. The pretensions of the Austrian house to universal empire and to suppression of Protestantism must be firmly resisted. Hence the alliance of the Protestant powers of Northern Europe——English, Dutch, Danish, Swedish, North German, with the nominally Catholic power of France; an alliance initiated by Henry and Elizabeth, and firmly pursued by Richelieu, Gustavus Adolphus, Mazarin, and Cromwell.

The Great Design of Henry was cut short by the assassin; and Elizabeth had died seven years before. But Henry lived to see the first act of the drama well played out. The year before his death, his firm ally Maurice of Nassau, the worthy successor of William the Silent, had extorted from the Spaniards the recognition of Dutch independence, and a truce for eleven years. These years were a lull in the storm. Nothing stirred in Europe. England under James, France under the miserable sycophants who preceded Richelieu, Spain under the apathy of the third Philip, Austria under her Rodolph and Matthias; all slumbered and all smouldered. The conflagration burst out in 1618, and it raged for thirty years. A vigorous hand, that of Ferdinand II, had grasped the Austrian Government, Maximilian of Bavaria seconding his policy; an ambitious minister, Olivarez, swayed the forces of Spain; Protestantism crushed in Styria, crushed in Bohemia, extinct in Bavaria, stripped of its old champions in England, Holland, and France, dependent on the feeble arm of Christian of Denmark, or on the miserable vacillations of John George of Saxony and George William of Brandenburg ; Wallenstein, like Attila the Scourge of God, carrying desolation and darkness from the Danube to the Baltic : such was the peril and the gloom of Europe during the first ten years of this tremendous war.

Two men stood out to face the storm : Gustavus Adolphus of Sweden and Cardinal de Richelieu. The two glorious years that Gustavus was permitted to give to the cause turned the tide of battle. Single-hearted, single-minded, and to the shame of Protestant Germany single-handed, his wise insight, his strong arm, and his noble devotion triumphed over the concentrated forces of his foes and the miserable cowardice of his friends. Fatally brief was his career, but his work survived him. Sweden remained till the end of the seventeenth century one of the great powers of Europe.

Gustavus, in his desperate march from the Baltic to the heart of Germany, was sustained by the moral support of France. Richelieu's grasp of the situation was indeed far larger, if not more noble, than that of the Swedish hero. Gustavus was inspired, as Cromwell after him, by something of the enthusiasm of the Protestant crusader. Richelieu, Cardinal of the Roman Catholic Church, was devoted to the interests of neither sect. His policy (if I may be permitted to repeat a word which sooner or later must find an accepted place in our language) was simply Occidental. I use the word in its double sense of contrast. His policy was Occidental, as opposed on the one hand to a purely national policy, and as opposed also to an exclusively Catholic or Protestant policy.

The pacification of Western Europe, as the essential
basis of all future progress, was his grand object.
To attain this object, two conditions were necessary :
first, no power in Europe must attain such territorial
magnitude as to intimidate the rest ; secondly, each
of the two religions must definitively abandon all hope
of victory over the other.    Both these conditions
Richelieu succeeded in fulfilling.

The first step then was to resist the dangerous
encroachments of the Spanish monarchy.    For the
first twenty years of the century, Spain, under the
feeble successor of Philip II, exhausted by the Dutch
rebellion, had ceased to threaten Europe.    But at
the death of Philip III, Olivarez succeeded to power,
and co-operated with Ferdinand of Austria for the
joint aggrandizement of the Spanish house.    How
ripe the time was for such efforts, how weak politically
were most of the Protestant nations, I have already
shown.

Richelieu had two great obstacles.    First, the
French Court, which under Anne of Austria and her
troop of intriguing traitors had become itself half
Spanish.    Secondly, the monstrous claims of the
French Protestants to become a self-governing republic in the State, to constitute in the most literal
sense an *imperium in imperio,* made it very difficult
to take any European action overtly favourable to
Protestantism.    Richelieu triumphed over both
obstacles.    He crushed the Spanish Queen and her
courtiers ; he crushed the political power, while pre-
serving the religious liberty, of the French Protestants;
and then he was free to act.    The year after he had
captured the great Protestant stronghold in France

(La Rochelle, 1628), he concluded his alliance with the great Protestant king. He secured English friendship, so far as it was then worth having, by the French marriage of Charles. He broke the territorial chain which united Spain with Austria ; a chain which extended continuously from North Italy through Western Switzerland to the Palatinate, and thence to the Lower Rhine. Leaving the contest on the Rhine to Gustavus's successor, Bernard of Saxe-Weimar, he shut off the Spanish Milanese from Austria, by supporting the Swiss Canton of the Grisons in their possession of the Valtellina ; he protected Louis of Nevers in his claim to the Duchies of Montferrat and Mantua ; and by the capture of Pignerol, the frontier fortress between France and Piedmont, he kept Savoy in check. But he carefully avoided falling into the error of Francis I and his successors. Annexation of the Italian soil, or of any part of it, to France, was no part of his plan. 'While Spain holds Italy, France,' he said, ' must occupy the gates of Italy ; Italy itself she does not want.' The direct attack on Spain was made where she was most vulnerable, in Rousillon and Flanders ; and, a few months after his death, the great victory of Rocroi (1643) morally decided the contest. He died before the contest was over ; but the school of statesmen which he had formed, the Serviens, the Lyonnes, and the Mazarins, found the rest of their work comparatively easy. The treaty of Westphalia abolished the supremacy of the Austrian house in Germany ; it put an end for ever to the religious wars ; it secured the liberties of Northern Protestant Germany against Southern

Germany, imperial and Catholic ; it secularized many
of the monstrous German bishoprics ; and, above all,
it established the great international principle, that
no one power in Europe should be permitted to over-
shadow the rest.   We shall see that France was the
first power to infringe this great principle, and to
incur the heaviest penalties for its infraction.

Pope Innocent x fulminated in vain despair
against this great treaty, so profoundly destructive
to the dearest principles of Catholicism ; less wise
in so fulminating perhaps, less amusing certainly,
than his predecessor, Urban VIII, who, when he heard
of Richelieu's death, contented himself, so Madame
de Motteville tells us, with a more equivocal con-
demnation : ' Se gli è un Dio,' he said, 'lo pagarà :
ma se non ci è Dio, veramente galantuomo.'   (If
there is a God, he will have to smart for what he has
done ; but, if there is no God, he was certainly an
excellent man.) [1]

Two points may be questioned in Richelieu's
foreign policy.   His wars were very costly ; and
they left behind them a legacy of immense financial
difficulties.   Were they worth the cost ?   France
acquired by the war Alsace with the exception of
Strasburg, and certain points of Lorraine.   Was this
acquisition dangerous to the peace of Europe ?

To the first objection I will quote the words of
Voiture, a contemporary writer who had been for a
long time a strenuous opponent of Richelieu's policy.
' When, two hundred years hence,' he says, ' those
who come after us read the history of this time ; if
they have a drop of French blood in their veins,

[1] De Motteville, vol. i, p. 115.

any love for the honour of their country, can they
read of the great things which he has done without
love and admiration ?  And will they, think you, love
or esteem him less because the national debts were
not paid quite as regularly as they should be ?    All
great things cost high ; but we must consider that
States are immortal, and we must think of the gain
to future generations as though it were already
present.' [1]

His wars were necessary, I repeat, to the salvation
of Europe ; the salvation of that which is its life, its
spiritual freedom.    On them depended whether
German Protestantism should be crushed, whether
Dutch liberty should be maintained : indirectly
English freedom, as Cromwell well knew, was at
stake also.    Nor can the French acquisitions in
Alsace and Lorraine, whatever their motives, and
these must be judged relatively to the standard of
that age, be justly censured on the ground of being
inconsistent with the peace of Europe.    It was
essential that France, no more than Spain, should be
enabled to trample upon Europe ; but that France
should be a strong power in Europe was vital, so at
least it seems to me, to the interests of the human
race.    Nominally Catholic, but possessing what was
ultimately far more essential to the liberties of
Europe than Protestantism itself ; possessing that
of which Holland, England, or Sweden knew little
more than Spain or Italy, the principle of religious
toleration contained in the Edict of Nantes,—it was
essential that France should be strong enough to

[1] Voiture's Correspondence, Letter lxxiv ; quoted in Martin's
*Histoire de France*, vol. xi, p. 441.

enrol that principle in the common law of Europe,
and to prevent its subsequent erasion.   France was
indeed destined to lapse deplorably from these great
traditions, and to become for a time the enemy and out-
law of Europe.   But deeply as she lapsed, all the more
splendidly did she rise again, under the great thinkers
of the eighteenth century, to the foremost place as
the champion of the spiritual liberties of the West.
And the glorious defence of their soil, which at the
close of the eighteenth century the French Republi-
cans maintained against the united kings and aristo-
cracies of Europe, would probably have been hopeless,
had the eastern boundary of France been less distant
from her capital.   Obviously no statesman, not even
the greatest, of the seventeenth century, is to be
judged by the standard of the nineteenth.   Richelieu,
we may be sure, looked forward to the conquest of
Alsace with a clear conscience.   He was unquestionably anxious to secure for his country a definite,
clearly defined boundary, analogous to that of
England or of Spain.   But the extravagant schemes
of Italian, Spanish, or Belgian conquest, by which
Francis the First before him, and Louis XIV and
Napoleon afterwards were seduced and ruined, were
to him utterly repugnant.

And these traditions of moderation he bequeathed
to his successor Mazarin.   By him they were scrupulously observed, both in the treaty of Westphalia, and
in the treaty of the Pyrenees with Spain eleven years
afterwards.   For Spain persisted in the war so long
after Austria had given it up as hopeless.   Unwise
as such persistence was, she was encouraged in it by
the civil war of the Fronde, described in my last

Lecture, and by the recklessness with which the aristocratic leaders of the Fronde tampered with Spain to serve their party. In 1650, the two greatest generals of France, Turenne and Condé, had for a time coalesced with Spain ; and Condé, the victor of Rocroi, continued to lead the Spanish armies till the peace. Mazarin's firm persistence in the war in spite of these internal obstacles, his firm refusal to yield to conditions dictated by an alliance of enemies without with traitors within, deserves high praise. Mazarin, like Richelieu and Henry IV, sought his friends among the Protestant powers. Firm alliance with republican England and its great Protector, with the Dutch Republic, with Christina of Sweden and her successor, and with the Protestant powers of Germany, ultimately incorporating into the alliance Bavaria and other of its Catholic princes also ; such was Mazarin's policy, and it proved successful. By the treaty of 1659, peace was restored to Europe ; the Pyrenees were fixed as the northern limit of Spain, and a daughter of Philip IV became the Queen of France.

Mazarin died two years afterwards. His reckless avarice, his fortune of five millions sterling, whence and how collected it was impossible to know, and only too easy to guess, the wiliness and suppleness of his nature, are not to blind us to his steady devotion to a policy framed and followed in the interests of his adopted country, and of Europe. Well for that country, and for Europe, had the statesmen of France for the next four generations been men of equal moderation and wisdom.

With the death of Mazarin in 1661 the reign of

H

Louis XIV begins.    Internally, as we have seen, it
was for many years the dictatorship, not of Louis XIV,
but of Colbert.    In foreign policy Louis assumed,
subject to the influences hereafter to be noticed, a
bolder and more personal initiative.    In the memoirs
drawn up by his own hand for the benefit of his
son, he describes clearly enough the relations of
France with the different powers of Europe at the
time when he resolved to take the government into
his own hands.    In this review it may be useful for
us to follow him.    Placing ourselves by the side of
King Louis in 1661, the year of Mazarin's death
and Louis's accession, we may glance rapidly at the
political condition of the powers of Europe.

Let us begin with the Northern powers, with whom
it had been the policy of France now for more than
seventy years to unite her action.    We find England,
after the convulsions of her civil war, after the
strong tension of Cromwell's government, on the
verge of powerless and ignominious collapse.
Elizabeth had given England a proud place in
the councils of Europe ; and at her death the
great Henry of France felt that he had lost his
strongest hope.    From her death (in 1603) to the
death of Charles I, England had been a cipher in the
European State-system.    The impotent attempt of
Charles I and Buckingham to assist the French
Protestants in their causeless rebellion had ended
as it deserved.    The part taken by the Stuarts in
the Thirty Years' War was utterly insignificant.
James had failed wholly in protecting the interests
of his son-in-law, the Elector Palatine ; and the
marriage of Charles I with a French Princess was

the sole service which Richelieu in the pursuit of his great policy could extract from England.

But, after an interval of half a century, England was again governed strongly and wisely. Under Cromwell her name was feared and honoured throughout Europe. His policy, with few deviations, was that of the great French statesmen; alliance with France and with the Northern powers for the peace of Europe. The brief war with Holland, and the unforewarned attack on Spain, are blots upon his foreign policy. For the first, he was not perhaps fully responsible; for the second, the war with Spain, he cannot be held guiltless; and it has to be noticed as one of the first in a series of unjust English wars, a series which has not yet ceased, for which no other motive can be assigned than that of commercial aggrandizement. On the whole, however, Cromwell's foreign policy, like that of Richelieu and Mazarin, tended to that which was the necessary condition of European progress—peace, equilibrium of powers, and resistance to religious tyranny. Cromwell died two years before Mazarin; and Louis XIV had to deal for the next twenty years with the contemptible government of Charles II. From England, then, for a wise governor of France, there was little to be hoped or feared.

From England let us pass to the Northern continental powers; and first, to the Dutch Republic. It was now eighty years since the seventeen provinces of the Netherlands, which Mary of Burgundy had brought as a dowry to Maximilian of Austria, and which Charles V at his abdication bequeathed to Philip of Spain, had been finally divided. By the

Union of Utrecht, in 1579, the five provinces of
Holland, Zealand, Utrecht, Guelderland, and Fries-
land declared their political independence ; Overyssel
and Groningen subsequently joined them, and the
Republic of the Seven United Provinces was thence-
forth one of the powers of Europe.    There are
pages in its short history of a splendour that the
annals of no other nation can surpass.    To find a
parallel to the struggle of William the Silent against
the overwhelming forces and generalship of Spain,
we must go back to the days of Marathon, or forward
to the defence of the French Republic against the
kings of Europe.    It was a struggle worthy of the
men whose ancestors in far distant ages had won
from the ocean the very soil they trod.    It was a
struggle for the imitation of their descendants a
century afterwards, when France had become for
a generation the retrograde power in Europe, and
Louis XIV had occupied the place of Philip of Spain.

The formation of the Dutch Republic was an
event of vast importance in Europe.    It was a blow
to feudalism.    It initiated the tradition of modern
Republicanism, which, passing on to England and
thence to our American colonies, found a far larger
and completer fulfilment in the French Republic
established in 1792 ; which still, under whatever
monarchical, constitutional, or imperial disguises,
remains undestroyed, nay, rather is far more vital
than at its first formation.    It is needless to point
out the essential difference between the Republic
of the United Provinces and the municipal republics
of Germany or Northern Italy.    Some of these had
existed from the times of the Roman Empire, or

from the earliest of the Middle Ages. Their historical importance is very great ; and their contagious influence helped to bring about what is unquestionably the greatest event in mediæval history, the rise of the chartered boroughs in the eleventh and twelfth centuries. But Republicanism within the walls of Hamburg or Florence was not incompatible with feudalism outside. It meant little more than municipal self-government. The free cities of Germany recognised the supreme authority of the Emperor ; and even in Italy, as the energetic appeals of Dante show, this authority never wholly disappeared. Dante's ultimate hope for Florence was the reassertion of imperial authority by the German Emperors—Albert or Henry VII. The republics of the Middle Ages had free institutions within their walls ; outside them, the divine right of kings or nobles remained unshaken.

The Republicanism again of ancient Greece or Rome differed from the modern conception of the word still more widely. It is sufficient to allude to the fundamental fact, that in the Greek or Roman States, even in the most democratic, the free citizens constituted a pure aristocracy, the vast mass of the working population being slaves. From Athens and Rome to the free towns of the Middle Ages, a stride had been taken of incalculable importance in human progress ; the personal freedom of the working classes.

But the Republic of the Seven United Provinces was, so far as it went, a still further step in advance. It aimed at something more than municipal freedom and religious toleration within the walls of certain

towns.  It was a direct attack on the feudal constitution of Europe.  It attacked simultaneously the
two elements of feudalism, royalty and aristocracy.
Not merely did it raise the *tiers état*, the commonalty, to collateral power with the aristocratic
class, but it tended to extinguish that class altogether.
It abolished the Church too as a State institution.
Of the three estates of which, till the French
Revolution, the political fabric of European society
consisted, clergy, nobility, commonalty, it left but
the last standing.  To the conception which is the
essence of modern Republicanism, that the whole
force of the State shall be devoted to the public
welfare, the Dutch Revolution of 1579 was a first
and a most important, though very imperfect,
approximation.

One feudal element was still suffered to exist ;
the hereditary influence of the House of Orange.
It was an influence against which the pure Re-
publicans strove constantly, and which during the
seventeenth century continued to be a constant
source of disturbance.  Yet it was compensated in
part by the remarkable character of three members
of that house : William the Silent, to whom the
formation of the Dutch Republic is due ; Maurice,
his son, whose masterly skill in warfare defended it
for twenty-two years against the Spanish power ;
and William, his great-grandson, the third William
of the house of Nassau, the third also of England.
At the time we are speaking of, William III of
Orange was eleven years old.  The Republican
party was in the ascendant.  His father, William II,
was dead ; and Cromwell, fearing the monarchical

tendencies of the family, made stronger by its alliance with the family of Stuart, had used strong pressure with the Dutch Government to induce them to exclude for ever from the Stadtholdership all members of the house of Orange.

From Holland then, as from England, there was nothing to fear. For eighty years she had been the firm ally of France. Commercially, their mutual relations were most valuable to both. The Dutch conducted the carrying trade of France, as, until Cromwell's navigation laws, they had conducted it for England : they imported what she required for home consumption, they exported her fine cloths, her corn and wine. In religion the relation was less close. The bitter Calvinism of the Dutch did not reciprocate the toleration which France still afforded to Protestants. The Catholic worship was wholly suppressed in Holland. Yet Henry IV, Richelieu, and Mazarin had found this difference compatible with firm alliance. For a wise statesman the policy of France to Holland was clearly marked out by such predecessors.

Passing from Holland to Sweden, Louis still found a firm, a sure, and a powerful ally. The great Gustavus, I have said, had left his work behind him. His great generals, Bernard of Saxe-Weimar, Banér, Torstensson, maintained the balance of military skill against Spain, till young Condé could destroy the Spanish infantry at Rocroi. In statesmanship, Oxenstiern, superior to his master, was both worthy and willing to co-operate with Richelieu ; and Sweden was left at the treaty of Westphalia the firm ally of France, secure as yet from the

aggressions of Russia, with a strong hold on the
Baltic shores of Germany, and unquestionably the
most powerful State in Northern Europe.

Passing to Germany, Louis would find the omens
not less favourable.    It was to the efforts of
Richelieu and Mazarin that Northern Protestant
Germany owed its independence of Southern Catholic
Germany.    And by the treaty of Westphalia, the
links that bound together the cumbrous unity of
German empire had been weakened, though not
shattered.    Germany had become, what France
would have become if its aristocracy had had their
way, a shapeless collection of half-detached States ;
their disunion paralysing all common action, their
nominal union under the Austrian shadow a hopeless
obstacle to the vigorous vitality of smaller isolated
States.    Disastrous to Germany has been the hollow
prestige, so unwillingly, so recently abandoned, of
the Holy Roman Empire.    To it, far more than to
any fancied peculiarity of race, we must attribute
the singular absence of political capacity which
marks them from the other nations of the West.
Disastrous to Germany ; to Europe perhaps not
equally disastrous.    As in the small republics of
Greece, as in the small states of Italy, great minds,
finding no political career worthy their acceptance,
have withdrawn themselves into regions of thought
more abstruse or more congenial ; and to the
impossibility of statesmen Germany owes perhaps
her artists and her thinkers, whose work has been
European, and not purely national.[1]

With Germany, Richelieu's successor, Mazarin,

[1] See Note appended to this Lecture.

had found it easy to deal. He had found two confederations ; one Protestant, joined by Sweden, Brunswick, and Hesse-Cassel ; the other Catholic, formed of the ecclesiastical electors of Cologne, Trèves, Mainz, and the Elector of Bavaria. By the alliance of the Rhine (1658), his greatest diplomatic effort, Mazarin joined both these leagues into one. It was a solemn confirmation of the treaty of Westphalia ; a distinct stipulation with the Austrian house that they should preserve strict neutrality in the struggle between France and Spain ; that they should prevent all revival of the Thirty Years' War. Germany then was at peace with France, and was likely to remain at peace.

Cross the Alps : what dangers were there for Louis, or what temptations ? Italy, like Germany, had been condemned from the Middle Ages to political insignificance, and from a stronger reason. For the very existence of Catholicism, as a spiritual power antagonistic to Feudalism, and modifying the oppressiveness of the military feudal caste, a certain admixture of temporal power was necessary. Relatively to the constitution of society in the Middle Ages, it was necessary that the Pope should be, not indeed a king or emperor, but an independent prince, protected by the greater powers, yet not subordinate to any one of them. The necessity was deplorable ; and by Dante, as by Ariosto and other Italian thinkers, it was bitterly deplored. But the necessity unquestionably existed if the Head of Catholicism was to wield any real spiritual power at all ; if he was to be anything more than a creature of the nearest powerful state ; if he was to be

anything more respectable than a Russian Patriarch
or an Archbishop of Canterbury. The effect of the
Papal Principality in Italy was to condemn that
country to long years of political division, distraction,
and suffering. Those who agree with me in regarding the Papal power as the principal civilizing
influence in Europe between the tenth and thirteenth
centuries, will think that even that suffering was not
too dear a price. There was, too, as in Germany,
and to a very far greater extent, a weighty compensation. Her higher minds were driven from
politics into philosophy and art ; and the movement
of Humanity was quickened, or at least not slackened,
by the national loss.

In the sixteenth century, Italy had been the
spoil of Europe, and the bane of French kings. The
disastrous prize of spoliation had fallen to Spain.
On France, the bitter lesson of Pavia had not been
lost. Richelieu, as I have said, had in his struggle
with Spain held the 'gates of Italy,' so that Spanish
soldiers should not pass ; but of Italian soil neither
he nor Mazarin coveted an acre. And if Louis XIV
passed the Italian states in review, he had no reason
to be dissatisfied. Savoy had been terrified by
Richelieu into neutrality ; Mantua had been Richelieu's protégé ; Parma, Modena, and Tuscany were
firm friends ; Venice, in her sea entrenchments,
defiant and defensive against Spain and Austria,
had always been allied to France. Pope Alexander
VII, hostile personally to Mazarin, was neutral or
insignificant. Spanish Italy alone, the Milanese and
the two Sicilies, remained doubtful.

Turn now to Spain. The culminating point of

her power had been reached eighty years before, when her Italian possessions had been undisturbed for half a century ; when she still claimed the Netherlands, and when the seizure of Portugal had given her the undivided Peninsula, and the undivided sway of the Western and the Eastern Indies. But the acme of her grandeur was the point of sudden and sure decline. Europe had united against her. Holland spoiled her of half the Netherlands, threatened the other half, and stripped her of her Indian colonies. France menaced her Belgian frontier, and by the victory of Rocroi had destroyed the prestige of her infantry. England had robbed her of Dunkirk and Jamaica ; and Portugal, after sixty years of submission, had recovered her independence (1640). Finally, Spain had deliberately sacrificed her intellect and her energies to the altar of the retrograde faith. The rest of Europe might go where it would, to material prosperity, to scepticism, to revolution, to Chaos. Spain chose rather to abide by the old ship, wrecked though it might be. If the fortunes of the Church were failing, if the battle was a losing battle, so much the more reason to fight on. *Victrix causa Diis placuit, sed victa Catoni.* The cost she had well counted. Abandonment of intellectual or material progress, erasion of her name from the great powers of Europe, was not too high a price for the honour of standing last and alone in the rearward of a desperate retreat. In the past were at least chivalrous and saintly memories ; in the future was blank Chaos, or Paradises of coarse comfort, loveless and faithless. To any god or goddess that the next two centuries offered for her worship, she preferred very

distinctly the Virgin Mary and the Saints.    Wrong
she may have been ; well, at least for Europe, it will
be said, that it was not all Spain.    Surely it was
well ; and well also for Europe, it may one day be
found, that it is not wholly Anglo-Saxon.

Spain thus, after the peace of the Pyrenees, muti-
lated in dominion, retrograde in faith, exhausted in
resources, ceased to be one of the great powers of
Europe, although the prestige of her greatness was
still far from gone ;  and in the survey which we
have supposed young Louis XIV to have taken of
his position in Europe, the Spanish horizon was the
only region where he could have seen the least
symptoms of foul weather.    Even there, indeed, was
but the shadow of danger ; and turn elsewhere he
might, to the north, east, or south, to England,
Scandinavia, Germany, or Italy, there was not even
the shadow.    Henry IV's ideal vision, and Richelieu's
long life-labour, seemed on the brink of rich and full
accomplishment.    There was peace in Europe in
1660.    What was wanting to make that peace perpetual ?    Why was that hope to be deferred for three
half centuries ?

Yet in the fifty-six years between the peace of
the Pyrenees in 1659 and the death of Louis in
1715, there were four general wars, occupying thirty-
two years, or two-thirds of the whole.    The war
with Spain for the Belgian Succession, 1667-8 ; the
war with Spain and Holland, 1672-8 ; the war with
Spain, Germany, Holland, Savoy, and England,
ending with the peace of Ryswick, 1697 ; and the
war of the Spanish Succession, with England, Holland  Austria, Portugal, and Savoy, from  1700 to

1713. Of the hundred years that followed, from the death of Louis to the treaty of Vienna in 1815, France was at war for forty-four. Since that time, if we except the short expedition to Sebastopol, and the Italian campaign of 1859, there has been half a century of peace.[1]

What is the explanation of these wars? Are we to attribute them purely to the foolish and extravagant ambition of despotic rulers? Or were there any deeper and more general causes at work, rendering the vision of the great Henry difficult or impossible to realize? The answer to this question implies that we possess a clear conception of the part that War has played in the history of Man. It is well to realize that the *natural* state of man, as Hobbes long ago pointed out, is a state of war. The nineteenth century ideal of enlightened self-interest and peaceable money-getting is no ideal at all to the primitive savage. Wealth and comfort, as he understands those words, are no doubt objects of desire to him; but gratification of the combative instincts for their own sake is even more desirable. It is neither probable, nor on the whole is it desirable, that those instincts should ever become atrophied, although the modern direction given to them may be different. But in the ancient world, even in the highly developed states of Greece and Rome, fighting was the highest and noblest of all occupations. The work of the mechanic or the merchant was for the slave. War was the business of freemen. The whole scheme of society was based upon this. War brought conquest;

---

[1] [Within five years after the publication of these Lectures France passed through the catastrophe of the German war of 1870-1.]

conquest brought slaves to support the warriors.
The peculiar greatness of Rome among all the
ancient States was that she made war subservient to
peace ; that she incorporated the conquered nations
into her imperial organization. *Pax Romana*, the
peace of the Roman Empire, was the basis of the
modern industrial system.     The wars of mediæval
Europe were, as I have said, not wars of aggression,
but of defence against attacks from the outside ;
although the military caste was still supreme.     The
body politic of Western Europe was held together,
and to a great extent protected from internal dis-
cord, by the spiritual power of Catholicism.     But
when the power of the Popes yielded, in the fourteenth century, to the power of the kings, international dissensions broke out at once.     The English
invasion of France was one of the first symptoms of
this.     In the transition period of the last four
centuries, with the old Catholic-Feudal system
crumbling away, but with many of its worst elements
still existing, and the new scientific industrial system
very immature, there were, independently of the personal ambition of rulers, two distinct influences
always tending to war : religious differences, and
commercial, above all colonial, rivalry.     To the first,
we may attribute most of the wars of the sixteenth
century, to the second those of the eighteenth.     For
the first, the two powers most responsible were
Austria and Spain ; for the second, England.     In
the wars of the seventeenth century, considerations
of personal ambition and national aggrandizement,
whether in Spain or France, played a more distinct
part than in those of the centuries following or pre-

ceding; but neither of the other two causes were wanting.

The invasion of Holland in 1672 was the turning point in Louis XIV's career. Up to that time he had governed France, or at least had energetically assisted Colbert in governing it, well and wisely. The Government had brought order out of financial chaos, had checked feudal abuses, had removed innumerable obstructions to internal trade, and in every way had promoted the industrial interests of the country. In Colbert's policy there was but one ominous feature. Following the example given by Cromwell's government ten years before, he had instituted Navigation Laws. His reasons were the same as those of Cromwell; and they were reasons which, even in his time, Adam Smith considered sufficient to justify an infringement of free-trade principles. Cromwell and Colbert both wished for a fleet to defend their shores and their colonies. Without a commercial marine, a navy is impossible; and therefore it was that Colbert, like Cromwell, wished to give a factitious stimulus to the national carrying trade, which previously had been in France almost entirely, and to a great extent in England also, in the hands of the Dutch. The experiment in both countries was for the time successful. The commercial marine of both countries took a rapid stride; and both secured a rich recruiting ground for their navies. But it was very certain that commerce, carried on with such principles, would, just in proportion to its prosperity and its extent, promote sooner or later the very hostile contact against which it would seem intended as a remedy. The commercial and colonial wars of the eighteenth century proved this abundantly.

But though Colbert's policy, this point excepted, was essentially peaceful and progressive, there was an opposite influence at work before which he was destined to succumb. I speak of the spirit of religious reaction, organized and embodied in the order of the Jesuits. That remarkable body, of which no candid and philosophical appreciation has ever yet appeared, had undertaken the defence and political restoration of Catholicism now for more than a century. Their task was of course hopeless ; and after the first generation the wisest and best of the order had fully recognised its hopelessness. All that was noble and great amongst them (and let it be hoped that we shall soon recognise how much that was) had betaken themselves to missions in America, India, or China, where their very failures shine side by side with the alleged success of other sects.

Those who remained in Europe were in every respect inferior, intellectually and morally. In Europe their influence was, it must be said, due justice being done to their useful efforts in education, irritating, unsettling, and noxious. They had devoted themselves hitherto to Spain, as the most important and most hopeful of European powers. That motive led them now to the Court of France. France was now the only strong power in Europe ; a Catholic reaction in France was the sole chance of securing the ultimate victory of their cause. With their efforts in England under the Stuarts we are all sufficiently familiar. Of the English Government at least they thought themselves secure.

But their one great obstacle was the Dutch Republic. Its Republicanism was more fatal to them than its Calvinism. Holland was the most important centre of free thought in Europe. Spinoza had been born there. Descartes had lived there twenty years. Bayle could live nowhere else. Every attack on the orthodox system, whether in Church or State, could be published in Holland. The extraordinary number of French books published in the seventeenth and beginning of the eighteenth century in Amsterdam illustrate the mental activity of the country. Holland was just then the centre of the Revolution; a word not invented as yet in its abstract sense; but as a thing, as a force, perfectly well felt by the acute instincts of the Jesuit mind. There can be no question that the same influence which was brought to bear on Louis XIV's mind, with the view of expelling the Protestants from France, also wrought strongly in favour of the Dutch war. Had Louis been a stronger man, that influence might have worked in vain. But there were fatal weaknesses in his character, fatal defects in his training, likely to make him the slave of religious terrors. It would compensate, they told him, for the stains of his private life, for the scandalous obtrusiveness of his adulteries, if he turned the vast power he wielded to the interests of the Church. Subtle appeals to his vanity, to his weakness for military fame, and again to his fear of republican disturbance, were, we may be sure, not wanting.

It is no part of my aim in these Lectures to describe military campaigns. Voltaire's admirable *résumé* is sufficient for most readers. The pompous apparatus of war ; the union of the splendid talents of Condé and Turenne ; the passage of the Rhine with 100,000 men ; the capture of city after city ; the agitated terror of the Dutch capital, brought face to face with political annihilation ; the resolution, should all fail, to take to their ships and transport their country, except the soil of it, to Batavia ; the desperate and strong defence ; the dikes opened ; the submersion of large provinces throughout the long winter ; the sea fights with the united fleets of England and France ; the fury of the fierce democracy, and the tragic death of the De Witts, powerless to wield it to their will ; the stern defiance of young William of Orange, who can do one thing at least, if no other, 'die in the last ditch rather than see the ruin of his country' ; or who answers the insolent summons of the French King, that 'he shall know one day what it is to have offended a Prince of Orange' ; the expulsion of the vast army after two short campaigns : these things are known to all whose blood rises at the names of Marathon or Salamis, of Morgarten, Bannockburn, or Valmy.

Ignominiously repulsed in Holland, Louis found some compensation in attacking Spain, who, with her scattered incoherent dominion, was now 'the sick man of Europe.' Five years previous to the Dutch war, John De Witt, the wisest statesman of his time, had proposed that the Spanish Netherlands should be made an independent State under the joint protection of France and Holland. The wisdom of this plan was evident, both from the

Dutch and from the European point of view. This being unacceptable, the next best plan was an equitable division of Belgium between the two countries. Louis rejected both offers with scorn. 'What have these traders,' he said, 'usurpers themselves, to do with settling the interests of the two great kings of Christendom?' He had invaded the Spanish Netherlands in 1667, and taken Lisle and other important frontier towns. He had also occupied Franche-Comté, but had been compelled, at the treaty of Aix-la-Chapelle, to restore it. He now occupied Franche-Comté permanently. The last relic of the old Burgundian rivalry was thus cleared away, and France gained, at the treaty of Nimeguen, 1678, the boundary of the Jura mountains. It must be admitted, I think, that this acquisition, which seems to have been accepted most willingly by the population of the province, was not inconsistent with the peace and equilibrium of Europe.

But it began now to be evident to all the world that France was embarking in a retrograde career, dangerous alike to the political and to the spiritual freedom of Europe. The Jesuits were becoming supreme in France; one by one the tolerant provisions of the Edict of Nantes disappeared, and the time for its entire repeal was evidently approaching. An unscrupulous and ambitious war minister, Louvois, directed the French armies; and the seizure of Strasburg, three years after the treaty of Nimeguen, without provocation or excuse in a time of peace (1681), the occupation of Luxemburg, and the monstrous bombardment of Genoa (1684), showed

that a successor to Philip of Spain had arisen in
France.

And now came into play the machinery which
Richelieu and his great school of diplomatists had
set in motion half a century before.   The treaty of
Westphalia stood then as a standard of international
law, a basis upon which the statesmen of all
countries could negotiate.   In that treaty, and in
the treaty of the Pyrenees, the immediate sufferers
had been Spain and Austria ; but the principle
underlying those treaties had been that no power
should henceforward be allowed to gain overweening
preponderance in Europe ; and to this principle
Spain and Austria were now not slow to appeal.
The pressure of European diplomacy had been felt
by Louis in the treaties of Nimeguen and of Aix-la-
Chapelle, in which he had been forced to resign his
pretensions to Lorraine.   All the old allies of France
ranged themselves against her.   Holland, the first
to rise against Philip II, and bound to France by
every traditional tie, was now, under William III's
strong guidance, the very soul of the league against
her.   England, or rather the English Government, had hitherto been ignominiously subservient.
Charles II had sold Dunkirk to Louis (and in this,
without intending it, he had done well, for on that
side of the channel England should have no place) ;
he had been bribed by the French Government into
complicity with the nefarious attack on Holland ;
and it was evident that he too and his brother were
under Jesuit influence.   It must be owned too that
the commercial jealousy of Holland, the spirit which
led Englishmen to engage in war with Spain and

France throughout the eighteenth century for colonial aggrandizement, induced the English to acquiesce in Charles's policy.

But before the end of the Dutch war the opposition to it had become intense. The Parliament had imperatively demanded the recall of English troops from French service in the Palatinate; Charles II had been forced into conciliating English feeling by marrying his niece Mary to the most formidable enemy of France; and England had co-operated, during the treaty of Nimeguen, in forcing France to restore many of her conquests. The current of English feeling during the five years' reign of James II, from 1683 to 1688, under the dominion of a Jesuit clique closely allied with that which in France was expelling and persecuting the Protestants, is well known. In 1688 the climax was reached, and the bubble burst. Louis stood absolutely alone in Europe, with an expelled king and a handful of conspiring Jesuits as his sole allies. The league against him, known as the League of Augsburg, was joined by Sweden, by the North German Protestants, by Bavaria, by the Emperor Leopold, and by Spain. Holland and England were, of course, not wanting. The very Pope had refused to support James in his insane attempts to subvert Protestantism, on the ground of his being a creature of Louis; and the Jesuit Peters stood in direct antagonism with the Papal Nuncio.

The blind and criminal folly that in the face of such a coalition pushed Louis into European war, can only be compared with the folly equally great and still more culpable because more personal, of

Napoleon's expeditions in Spain and Russia, a hundred and twenty years afterwards. The war lasted nine years. It brought few territorial changes. The chief event was the destruction at the battle of La Hogue of the French fleet,—the fleet which had been created with such marvellous activity by Colbert's son, the Marquis of Seignelai ; and which, at the battle of Beachy Head two years before, had with inferior numbers beaten the English and Dutch fleets united. The peace of Ryswick in 1697 restored to Spain some of her Belgian frontier towns ; it left France with territory but slightly diminished, but with disordered finance, with exorbitant taxation, with ruined industry. Her wisest men and best generals were gone. Turenne had died, and Condé had retired before the war began (1675). Colbert had not lived to see the revocation of the Edict of Nantes. Louvois, the great war minister, had died in 1691 ; Seignelai, the minister of marine, the year after ; Luxemburg, Louis's best general, in 1695. Catinat, by far the greatest general surviving, had not been thought sufficiently aristocratic to succeed him, and the incompetent Villeroi had taken his place. Many of the ablest officers had been proscribed as Protestants. Schomberg and Ruvigny had joined the ranks of William.

It was in this condition that France, governed now by a very small and dull clique of Jesuits, old women, and bigots, plunged, three years after the peace of Ryswick, into the most hopeless and foolish of her wars, the war of the Spanish Succession. Charles II of Spain being without children, appointed

Philip of Anjou, a grandson of the king of France, and brother to the heir to the throne, as his successor. The arrangement was not objectionable, provided only that proper security was given that the two crowns of France and Spain should never under any circumstances be united. By refusing to give such security, Louis a second time united Europe against him. England, loaded with the heavy debt, might have hung back ; but when, on the death of James II, Louis with blind fatuity persisted in recognising his son as heir to the English crown, she threw her whole weight into the anti-French league, joined, with the exception of Bavaria and Spain, by every power in Europe. Of that league Eugene and Marlborough were the arms ; Heinsius, grand pensionary of the Dutch Republic, was the animating spirit. The result could not be doubtful. At Blenheim and Ramillies and Oudenarde, the worst generals in Europe were arrayed against the best. A Marsin, a Tallard, a Villeroi, afforded excellent sport to a Eugene and a Marlborough.

The war was ended by the peace of Utrecht in 1713. It lasted twelve years, it should not have lasted six. As early as 1706, Louis offered reasonable terms of peace ; but the allies were now in their turn unreasonable. Nothing less than a partition of France was at one time talked of, and Louis was told, in answer to a second offer of peace in 1709, that if he wished for peace he must send his own armies into Spain, and assist them in driving his own grandson from his throne. It was in answer to these intolerable terms that Louis, rising in his old age to the memories of better days, issued the well-known appeal to the French nation : ' I have offered fair terms of peace,' he said ; ' but seeing that our enemies in their pretence to negotiate are palpably insincere, we have only to consider how to defend ourselves, and show them that France united can resist the united powers of Europe in their attempts, by fair means or by foul, to ruin her. All the ordinary sources of revenue are exhausted ; I come before you for your counsel and assistance, at a time when our very safety as a nation is at stake ; let us show our enemies that we are still not sunk so low but that we can force upon them such a peace as shall consist with our honour and with the good of Europe.' The glorious defeat of Malplaquet and the triumphant victory of Denain were the answer to this appeal. The overthrow of Marlborough and his party in 1710, the accession of a Tory government, and the consequent withdrawal of England from the war, were conducive to a general peace.

By the treaty of Utrecht in 1713, England secured her main object of ambition, the French colonies of Newfoundland and Acadia ; for England was already launched into that career of colonial aggression and aggrandizement afterwards to be continued by the elder and the younger Pitt, to which so many of the wars of the eighteenth century were due. The territory of France was undiminished : the Belgian frontier differed hardly at all from what it had been fifty years before. Spain was left to its Bourbon dynasty ; but her Italian possessions were much narrowed. Milan was given to Austria. Sicily was given to the Duke of Savoy. Prussia became for

the first time a kingdom.    Such were the alterations
on the map of Western Europe.    In Eastern Europe
important changes had taken place.    In the heat of
the French struggle, in the year of Oudenarde, the
battle of Pultowa had been fought.    Sweden dis-
appears from among the great powers of Europe ;
and Russian influence becomes from that time forward a prominent and a perturbing, because alien,
force in Western Europe.

Indeed it might appear as if there were only two
strong forces left in the world : the brute force of
Russia outside the Western Republic ;  the nobler
and mightier force of Great Britain within.    In
Germany, Spain, Italy, and France, the signs of
political vitality were few.    England, triumphant
and strong, was fast approaching an era of political
aggrandizement and material prosperity.    Her
splendid aristocracy headed by the elder Pitt, her
commerce and her industry soon to be developed by
Watt, Arkwright, and their fellows, seemed to assure
her the future of the world.    Yet there was a force
mightier than the brute force of Russian armies ;
subtler and not less mighty, than the forces of the
steam-engine, or than the lust for gold.    What that
force was I leave to the next Lecture.    Enough to
say, that France of the eighteenth century, starving
and bankrupt as she might be, was the centre of its
action.

NOTE ON THE GERMAN EMPIRE (p. 104)

These lectures were delivered before I had read
Mr. Bryce's valuable essay on the *Holy Roman*

*Empire.* It will be seen that I hardly share his belief in the importance and influence of this Institution during the Middle Ages. Interesting as it is to trace the length to which ancient institutions prolong their shadows, and conceal from view the living forces of the present, it is yet most desirable to distinguish shadows from substances. The semblance of Imperialism that survived through the Middle Ages, like the semblance of Republicanism that was preserved during the first two centuries of the Empire, disguised the real forces that were at work, and thus may possibly have made the transition from the old to the new easier. I am far from wishing to detract from the greatness of Charlemagne's or Otto's policy. Charlemagne stands out as one among the two or three greatest statesmen of the world. His influence, extending as it did over Italy, France, Spain, and Germany, is one of the leading facts in the history of European civilization. But the Ottonic empire, which Mr. Bryce most judiciously distinguishes from the Carlovingian, is of importance rather to German than to European history. In the first place, its power was limited to Germany and a portion of Italy. Even in Italy its power was always disputed ; and, except during the reigns of the first and third Otto, and of Henry III, was disputed successfully. Secondly, its duration as a strong central power even within this comparatively narrow radius was very brief. Founded in 962, it fell, as Mr. Bryce himself says, with Frederick II in 1250 ; 'emerging from the ruin indeed, and destined to a long life, but so shattered, crippled, and degraded, that it could never more be

to Germany and Europe what it once had been.'[1]
And even during these three centuries of comparative
vitality, it would be hard to select a hundred years
during which the power of the emperors in Italy was
more than nominal.

We should form, I think, a very inadequate conception of the great struggle of the Middle Ages if
we reduced it to a contest between the Papacy and
the Empire.    It was a contest between Catholicism
and Feudalism ; between the Popes as the representatives of the one spiritual power, and the various
representatives of feudalism in Germany, England,
France, and Spain.    The sort of honorary precedence given to the German monarch, and which to
contemporaries seemed of far greater consequence
than it was, must not blind us to the fact that a
struggle precisely identical with that between Pope
and Emperor was going on in other countries between Pope and King.    To Hildebrand the submission of William the Conqueror was not less
important than that of Henry IV.    In fact the
Emperors were by no means the most formidable
antagonists that the Popes had to meet.    The
strongest of the Emperors bowed lower, as the
porch of St. Mark still testifies, than the feeblest
of the Plantagenets.

With regard to the statement made in the text,
that the pretensions of Empire have resulted in the
disunion of Germany, Mr. Bryce and myself are
fully at one.    'Italy terribly avenged the wrongs
she suffered.    Those who destroyed the national
existence of another people, forfeited their own : the

[1] Bryce's *Holy Roman Empire*, 2nd edit. p. 231.

German kingdom, crushed beneath the weight of the Roman Empire, could never recover strength enough to form a compact and united monarchy, such as arose elsewhere in Europe.  The want of national union and political liberty from which Germany suffers, cannot be attributed to the difference of her races ; . . . rather is it due to the decline of the central government, which was induced by its strife with the Popedom, its endless Italian wars, and the passion for universal dominion, which made it the assailant of all the neighbouring countries.  The absence or weakness of the monarch enabled his feudal vassals to establish petty despotisms, debarring the nation from united political action, and greatly retarding the emancipation of the Commons. Thus, while the princes became shamelessly selfish, justifying their resistance to the throne as the defence of their own liberty,—liberty to oppress the subject, —and ready on the least occasion to throw themselves into the arms of France, their subjects were deprived of all political training, and find the loss of such experience baffles their efforts to this day.' [1]

[1] Bryce's *Holy Roman Empire*, pp. 418-19, 2nd edit.

# LECTURE IV

## PROGRESS OF THOUGHT DURING THE SEVENTEENTH CENTURY

FOR five centuries the system of thought and of life under which men had lived from the third century to the thirteenth, from St. Augustine and St. Ambrose to St. Bernard and St. Francis, has been crumbling to decay. The great institution of the Middle Ages, the power which, belonging to no country, to no caste, existing apart and distinct from the temporal power, could modify by the spiritual agencies of faith and opinion the physical force and brute selfishness of feudal tyranny, was already losing its vitality when Dante wrote his great poem. The Papacy was doomed, and the doom was in course of execution, two centuries before Luther began to fulminate. The Catholic structure fell because the dogmas upon which it rested were irreconcilable with the progress of modern thought. Ideas rule the world. It has been said that not ideas, but passions, desires, interests rule the world. Both, in a sense, are true. The ship is ruled by the helm ; it is driven by the winds or the steam-engine. Passion impels ; opinion guides.

The fabric of mediæval society rested upon a

basis of supernatural dogma. The acceptance of
such dogma proves no inferiority in the great
Catholic thinkers. If indeed the individuality of
Man were as complete and self-sufficing as many
writers of our time claim that it is, such powerful
minds, it may be thought, would have long ago
burst their shackles. But the mental evolution of
the human mind is to be studied in the collective
human race far more surely than in any isolated
member of it. To study a living organism apart
from its environment is now recognised by biologists
as an absurdity. In the case of the human being,
the environment to be studied is not merely physical,
but sociological. The higher aspects even of the life
of an animal cannot be studied without reference to
its social relations, simple as they may be ; limited,
in most cases, to the most elementary relations of the
family. In man the impossibility of comprehending
the individual apart from the society of which he is
a member, is incomparably more direct and certain.
In the lower tissues the isolated cell may be studied,
though even there most imperfectly ; but who would
profess to explain the actions of a single cell of
muscular or nervous substance? It would be easy
and fallacious to press this analogy too far. But it
may serve to represent, though in an exaggerated
form, the complicated influences which man exercises
over his fellow. The laws by which the evolution of
the human mind proceeds are the same for all ; but the
rapidity of growth is infinitely various ; and the movement of the stronger minds is affected in ways far more
intricate probably than we shall ever be able to analyse,
by the contagious inferiority of those around them.

In attempting then to explain the extraordinary difference in the mental framework of St. Bernard in the twelfth century, and of D'Alembert in the eighteenth, it is the collective evolution of society at those different periods that must be studied in the first instance ; differences in the individual leaders of thought being to so great an extent dependent on it.    It has been shown by Auguste Comte that all mental conceptions pass, or tend to pass, through three stages : in the first of which phenomena are attributed to the direct intervention of imaginary beings ; in the second it is sought to account for them by metaphysical abstractions ; and in the third it is not sought to account for them at all, but simply to study the laws or general methods of their succession or coexistence.    Take, as an instance, the simple phenomenon of the sleep produced by the action of opium on the human body.    The Arabs even in the present day are content to attribute it to the 'will of God.'[1]    Molière's medical student accounts for it by a 'soporific principle' contained in the opium.    The modern physiologist knows that he cannot account for it at all.    He can simply observe, analyse, and experiment upon the phenomena attending the action of the drug, and classify it with other agents analogous in character.

To this law of Evolution must be added the law of the rapidity with which different classes of conceptions tend to pass through these phases.    Other circumstances being equal, the rapidity varies with their complexity.    The simpler phenomena, those embraced in the sciences of geometry or astronomy,

[1] See Palgrave's *Travels in Arabia.*

are brought into the Positive stage first.   The more
complex, those of animal life, or of human society,
remain longest under the influence of supernatural or
metaphysical dogmas.   Thus the three methods of
philosophizing may coexist in the same mind in
different departments of thought, and in the same
department of thought in different minds.   In these
two laws, rightly understood, we have a clue which
goes far to unravel the complicated labyrinth of
European thought during the last two thousand
years.

Already in ancient Greece, under the influence
of the great thinkers of Athens and Alexandria, the
conception of invariable Law had been applied to
the simpler phenomena of the universe.   The more
complex were still left to the dominion of innumerable gods.   But Polytheism, under the impulse given
by Plato and Aristotle, the latter of whom was always
recognised by mediæval thinkers as their predecessor,
condensed itself into Monotheism ; and the conception of universal Law became now less difficult,
though still profoundly contradictory to the dominant faith.   The dogmas on which the spiritual
power of Catholicism rested became gradually in-
credible to the stronger minds.   The central dogma,
above all, the belief in Transubstantiation, which,
by bringing men weekly and daily into contact with
the region of miracle, accustomed them to the idea
of constant supernatural intervention, was undermined deeply by the celebrated controversy between
the Nominalists and Realists in the thirteenth century.
That controversy disposed men to content themselves
with studying phenomena, the facts of the universe as

they appear to our limited and imperfect senses, and
to abandon the discussion about hidden and underlying causes as inscrutable, and therefore useless.

And while these changes were taking place in the
world of thought, changes of equal importance were
going on in the world of common life. The rise of
the modern industrial system, the enfranchisement
of the boroughs, the contact with Asiatic countries
in the Crusades, the great discoveries of the compass,
of paper, of printing, of gunpowder, the limitation of
the military spirit by the formation of standing armies,
the evident fact that peaceful industry was henceforth
to be substituted for war as the permanent occupation of free men,—all these things had gone far to
shatter the old system, and contained in themselves
the germs, undeveloped as yet, of the new. During
the fourteenth and fifteenth centuries the Papal power,
neutralized by schisms, heresies, and general councils,
became in almost every country in Europe wholly
subordinate to the civil power. In the sixteenth
century the destruction went on far more systematically and rapidly. The audacious speculations
of Copernicus, the Renaissance of classical art and
literature in Italy, made less noise perhaps, but
were of even greater permanent importance than
the religious insurrection of Luther, consolidated
by the systematizing genius of Calvin. By the
Protestant movement Catholicism was shorn of half
its dimensions. Whether that movement has proved
so favourable to the permanent progress of the
human mind as is generally thought, is a question
open to grave doubts. Of this I shall have more
to say afterwards. But its immediate effect on

K

the intellect of Northern Europe was strongly to stimulate the growth of literature, art, and science, which hitherto had been almost limited to the South.

In the confused and tangled course of modern history it is useful, as I have before said, to distinguish two processes, which bear mutually upon one another, but which yet are separate : the decomposition of the old ; the composition of the new. It is obvious, in the first place, that the former movement has always proceeded, or rather has always tended to proceed, far more rapidly than the latter. From Wycliffe and Huss to Luther, from Luther to Calvin, from Calvin to Socinus ; from the Unitarianism of Socinus to the Deism of Voltaire, and still onward to the complete negativism of D'Alembert and Diderot, the logical steps seem easy and rapid. Reading the great Italian and French writers of the sixteenth century,—Ariosto, Rabelais, Montaigne, we seem on the very verge of that mighty revolution which yet was not to burst out till two centuries afterwards. The destruction of the authority of the Church, and of the daily miracle of the Mass, seems at first sight as if it involved prompt and speedy destruction of all the rest ; and this, with many isolated minds, was assuredly the case.

Meantime the constructive movement had been going on far more slowly. The system under which men had lived for centuries was breaking up ; the system under which they were to live for the future was hardly visible. The rules of life, of duty, of right and wrong, had been based hitherto on a structure of supernatural faith. That structure having given way, the problem for men to solve was how to frame a scheme of life, a standard of duty, based on the foundation which it was clear could for the future be the only firm foundation, that of scientific thought. The problem then was, stated in other words, how to bring the moral and social relations of men within the sphere of Positive Science. Towards the solution of this mighty problem most of the great thinkers of Western Europe, during the last three centuries, have, in ways more or less imperfect, each in their special department, been labouring.

But in the sixteenth century the approximations to it were but very slight. At a time when even the planets were supposed by most men to be under the dominion, not of regular laws, but of arbitrary spiritual influences, it was not likely that discovery of the laws of society and human development should be thought possible. The sciences of Physics, Chemistry, and Physiology still remained uncreated, or under the influence of the wildest metaphysical abstractions, except so far as the mechanical or medical arts connected with them had infused some positive notions of a practical or elementary kind. When the reason of a candle burning was said to be that it contained a large quantity of an inflammatory principle called phlogiston ; when philosophers thought they could explain the ultimate causes of heat and electricity by reference to imponderable and purely imaginary substances called caloric or electric fluids ; when the orbits of the planets were supposed to be necessarily circular because the circle is the most perfect of geometrical figures ; when the simplest facts of disease were accounted for by depression or exaltation of a mysterious something called the vital spirits, many of which delusions continued to haunt scientific men till the end of the eighteenth century, if indeed all of them are yet thoroughly extinct, it was not surprising that human affairs should be considered wholly beyond the reach of scientific law; and that those moralists and politicians who no longer believed in special interventions of the Deity, or in the divine right of kings, should still explain all social questions by reference to an imaginary entity called Nature, or by the metaphysical abstraction of the Rights of Man.

The condition, therefore, of men's minds during the greater part of modern history has been this. The ancient structure of thought and belief has been giving way, and has constantly seemed on the verge of utter dissolution; the materials for a new Synthesis, a new system, that is, of life, of belief, of duty, have been gradually and silently accumulating; but the process of accumulation has been very slow, and the putting together, the building up, the synthesis of these materials, has been very long delayed. But the nature of men and of human society is so constituted that utter anarchy is repugnant to it, and a long continuance of anarchy is wholly impossible. Isolated exceptions apart, men in the mass revolt, have always revolted, and will always revolt against Chaos. Rather than Chaos, they will tolerate the most slavish spiritual despotism, and cling to it as to an ark of refuge. Some principle to dominate conflicting passions, some bond other than self-interest to bind them to their fellow-men, some theory of life, some rule of action, men must and will have. Philosophers may chafe at this necessity, may strive impatiently to ignore it ; if they deserve the name, they will end by accepting it.

Consequently, ever since the sixteenth century, incessant attempts have been made, and are yet being made, to patch up the rents in the old system of thought, or, when this seemed plainly impossible, to construct some fresh system out of the fragments. The modes of these attempts were infinite. Protestantism, after its first revolutionary outburst, became consolidated in the hands of Melanchthon into Lutheranism ; by the organizing genius of the French reformers into Calvinism ; by English statesmen into Anglicanism. And the Catholic world had its own varieties of reconstruction too. Ignatius Loyola, Jansen, Pascal, Bossuet, Fénelon, each had his own conception of which fragment of the old to take up, which to reject ; how far to revive the past, how far to conciliate the future. Each of these men had his band of followers ; and the conflicts between them were frequent and fierce.

It will surely be allowed by every one, be he Protestant, Catholic, or sceptic, that the founders and co-operators of these partial and temporary reconstructions were for the most part men of no mean force and wisdom. In intellect, in energy, or in purity of character, Calvin and Ignatius Loyola were certainly not inferior to Voltaire or Rousseau. In singleness of purpose, and in mental calibre, Bossuet will certainly stand a fair comparison with Diderot. The insight of these men was amply sufficient to reveal to them the logical inconsequence of the

position they maintained ; their integrity and courage
was not inadequate to the effort of proclaiming it,
had it seemed desirable.    We stand face to face
here with a difficult problem.    Men have accounted
for the course taken by a Bossuet or a Cromwell by
supposing them imbecile, or by supposing them
hypocrites.    Either hypothesis is to me equally
untenable.    Strong sympathy with the spiritual, or,
if you prefer the word, with the moral necessities of
their fellow-men ; strong conviction of the utter
emptiness and misery of Irreligion, that is to say, of
spiritual anarchy ; of the hopelessness, while that
lasted, of a right solution of any social problem,
forced such minds as these to choose a practical
rather than a speculative career.    Leaving it to
others to continue the work of destruction, or to
dig deep into unpenetrated mines of truth, and
so prepare the way for future builders, they chose
rather to construct temporary shelter out of the ruins
of the old ; *faire de l'ordre avec le désordre*, to
organize, in however transient a way, the disorder
around them.

These considerations I should not have obtruded
had they not seemed to me absolutely necessary for
the understanding of what is the subject of this
Lecture, the movement of European thought during
the seventeenth century.    It was a century, by comparison with its predecessor and its successor, of
spiritual calm.    It stands midway between the century of the Reformation and the century of the
Revolution.    It partook, in its outward surface at
least, of the excitement of neither.    The religious
movement had spent its force ; Protestantism and

Catholicism were abandoning the struggle, or at
least abandoning all hope of victory in the struggle,
and were crystallizing as best they might into consolidated systems within their respective boundaries.
The revolutionary attack upon both was hidden as
yet in a future not distant, yet visible to few.    But
the calm of the seventeenth century was not stagnation.    Mighty changes were incubating ; revolutions of unheard of vastness were transacting ; not
in the forests of the New World, not in the Hall
of the Convention, not even in the wide-spreading
pages of the *Encyclopédie* or the *Contrat social*, but
in the silent depths of four or five mighty minds.

Four men, whose labours extend more or less
over the first generation of the seventeenth century,
were the leaders of this vast revolution — Kepler,
Galileo, Bacon, and Descartes.    The first two placed
the audacious hypothesis of Copernicus as to the
constitution of the universe within the pale of de-
monstrated science.    It is very hard for us to realize
the prodigious shock given by this new conception
to all the notions of man's position in the universe
that had become ingrained hereditarily from the first
origin of the human race.    The logical instinct of
the Catholic Church warned her of the danger.    Her
strenuous and futile persecution of Galileo shows
how keenly she felt it, and how impotent she was
to deal with it.    It was not merely the conflict of
the new discovery with the language of Genesis ;
that was but a small matter, with which the practical
wisdom of Catholic divines was fully competent to
deal.    It was the necessity of wholly shifting the
point of view from which man's position in the world

had hitherto been regarded.   He had been hitherto
the absolute centre of the universe : the sole and
special object of Divine intervention.   He now saw
himself and his planet to be an inconceivably insignificant atom, a mote in the sunbeam, a grain in
the sand - storm whirled in infinite space through
boundless years.   It was a complete and total transference of man's thoughts from the Absolute to the
Relative.   For in one sense, indeed, the old conception must remain for ever true.   Still, man must
remain to himself the centre of the universe ; but
the centre no longer absolute, but relative to the life
and well-being of his own race, to the past, present,
and future, of Humanity.

And what Kepler and Galileo did by their discoveries, that Bacon and Descartes did still more
thoroughly by their method.   The importance of
the third is perhaps even overrated in this country,
by comparison with the great thinkers of the
Continent.   He is spoken of too much as we speak
of Isaac Newton, as if he stood alone as the founder
of inductive philosophy.   Yet of the four men we
are speaking of, he is the one who did the least for
inductive philosophy with his own hands.   Not a
single important physical discovery is due to him.
It seems indeed surprising, when we think of the
time he gave to it, that he did so little.   His title
to fame rests on his strong grasp of two great truths:
first, that the intellect of the world must, and would
for the future, take a wholly different course from
that which it had previously taken ; that metaphysical inquiries into inscrutable causes must henceforth give way altogether to study of the laws of

phenomena, founded on observation and experiment ; secondly, that the exertions of the intellect must be bounded by considerations of human welfare, determined not in the spirit of narrow Utilitarianism, but in a large and far-sighted spirit.    In the *Novum Organum*, we have the germs of that subordination of intellectual effort to social and moral requirements which has brought the severe censure of scientific specialists upon the philosophical and political speculations of Auguste Comte.

But great as Bacon was, a still greater and more important figure in the intellectual movement of the seventeenth century was René Descartes.    Those who read his admirable discourse on *Method*, the value of which time will not impair, will see that he too had grasped the conception of organized and systematic exploration of the world around us with a power and effectiveness fully equal to that of Bacon.    Morally, he had the vast advantage over Bacon of being single-minded in the pursuit of the great mission which he had marked out for himself while yet a schoolboy.    The two great obstacles to the fulfilment of that mission, ambition of power or wealth, and literary vanity, he had put utterly aside. He fled from the interminable discussion, metaphysical pedantry, and intellectual conceit of the schools of Paris, to mix in utter obscurity with the world of practical life, where men, he said, reasoning about their own affairs and interests, were far more likely to reason vigorously and wisely.    As a soldier or as a traveller, he mixed with every phase of life in every country in Europe. Then he planted himself in Amsterdam, where every one but himself, as he observes with much satisfaction, being absorbed in trade, he might hope to work out his problems in that repose and perfect freedom from discussion, which was to him the one supreme blessing. In Holland he remained twenty years, studying geometry, physics, and anatomy, occasionally visiting the philosophical world of Paris. There he came into contact with Hobbes, Pascal, Fermat, Roberval, and others. He was there when the civil war of the Fronde broke out ; but the excitement of Paris was always too much for him, and after the day of the Barricades, in August, 1648, he left Paris never to return. Christina of Sweden invited him to Stockholm in 1649, where, in three months, the climate killed him in his 54th year.

His work can only be described as a synthesis of Positive Philosophy, so far as it was then possible. The grand object was, first to penetrate men with the conception, so wholly foreign to the modes of thinking then prevalent, of the existence of invariable laws in every department of nature; secondly, by the knowledge of these laws, to increase man's power over the world around him, and above all, over his own physical organization ; mastery over disease being to him a matter of even greater moment than increased power of producing wealth. His actual success in the different departments of this vast sphere was very unequal. But in every department he gave a stimulus to scientific thought far greater than that of Bacon ; and in his own special region of discovery, neither Bacon nor any other philosopher has rivalled him. His splendid generalization of geometrical method, commonly called the application of algebra to geometry, by which infinite numbers of problems, each formerly requiring a special study, were now solved by a miscellaneous process, is the starting-point of modern mathematics. In Physics his labours were not unfruitful, as his researches on light, and his explanation of the rainbow, sufficiently prove. The study of animal life, to which he devoted so many years, was less accessible to him. He was, perhaps, the first to accept and disseminate Harvey's great discovery, then recent, of the circulation of the blood. But the time for discovering the principal laws of vital phenomena had not yet come. What can be said is, that he gave a strong impulse in the right direction.

I spoke of his work as a synthesis of Positive Science. It was a synthesis inevitably imperfect. One domain, and that the most important, was left out, or rather was left to be treated not by positive but by metaphysical methods. The social and moral nature of man was not brought by him, and could not be brought, within the sphere of Positive Science. He did not neglect these subjects however. Indeed it is by this part of his labours that he is best known to the mere literary world. He dealt with the sphere of morality and religion by metaphysical as opposed to positive methods ; but his metaphysical writing, which gave the impulse successively to Locke, Leibnitz, Hume and his Scotch opponents, Kant and Kant's successors, was of the most formidable and destructive kind. To reduce all truth to the two ultimate axioms of God and of Consciousness, to make individual consciousness the

supreme test of truth, was a process at which
Catholic or Protestant divines might well shudder.
Descartes, anxious for repose as the one condition
of successful work, not feeling that the time for
doing the work of Diderot or Voltaire had come
yet, writing, as he distinctly tells us, not for his own
generation but for generations to come, was always
willing to profess conformity to the Church ; but no
outward conformity could compensate for a mode of
reasoning which, if followed out, led men inevitably
to make a clean sweep of the whole structure of
traditional belief, and begin again from the very
foundations.    Descartes had gone to Holland, hoping
to be left in quiet obscurity.    He was much mistaken.
The Calvinists dreaded his philosophy far more than
the Catholics.    The ministers of Utrecht, who had
been preaching zealously for the last ten years
against the discoveries of Galileo, now did all in
their power to imitate Galileo's persecutors.    It was
by a very narrow escape, due only to influential
friends, that Descartes escaped being convicted of
the charge of atheism, and having his books burnt
by the common hangman.    The Catholics, strange
to say, were far more lenient, and wiser in their
generation, though not perhaps wiser for the generation to come after them.    Trusting to the immense
power of resistance contained in the social fabric of
their Church, a power wholly independent of logic,
they met the danger boldly by adopting his
philosophy, fatal as it could not but prove to them
in the end.

I have gone somewhat more fully into the life
and work of Descartes, because he is to my mind not

only the most powerful, but the most representative intellect of the seventeenth century. From him more distinctly than from any other man we can trace the two great intellectual movements of the eighteenth and nineteenth centuries; the Critical philosophy and the Positive philosophy. The first, exposing the weakness of all such beliefs as from their nature are insusceptible either of proof or disproof, thus demarcated the knowable from the unknowable, and fixed the limits within which it is alone useful for the human intellect to exert itself; the second, building up within those limits a new structure of scientific conviction, formed a far securer basis than has ever existed before for the social and moral relations of man; it opened a new and wider sphere for his primæval instincts of Love, of Reverence, and of Duty.

Of these two great modern movements, Descartes is the first and most typical representative. I am not proposing to give you the history of philosophy or of science in the seventeenth century. I can but mention, in passing, his great co-operators in the critical movement, Hobbes, Spinoza, Malebranche, Locke, Leibnitz, Bayle. With their special opinions we can have little to do here. From the confused and tortuous conflict of their metaphysical speculations, one result shaped itself more and more clearly, the impossibility of metaphysics; and, as a consequence, the limitation of the human intellect to the sphere of Positive inquiry.

Meantime, while so much was being destroyed, much was being built up. The Critical philosophy was clearing the ground; the Positive philosophy

was rapidly preparing to occupy it.   Descartes and
Leibnitz stand out from all the other thinkers of the
seventeenth century as distinguished for equal services
in either field.   It was their privilege to build up as
well as to destroy.   They combined the work of
Newton and of Locke.   They were great scientific
discoverers as well as great metaphysicians.   Descartes took up the chain of geometrical discovery
where the Greek geometers, eighteen centuries before,
had left it off.   He generalized their methods by
reducing questions of quality to questions of quantity,
by showing that every kind of curved line could be
represented by an algebraic equation ; and thus
prepared the way for the greatest achievement of
modern science, due to the simultaneous efforts of
Leibnitz and Newton, the Infinitesimal Calculus.
These men pursued science with all the rigorous
exactitude and with more than the practical success
of the narrow scientific specialists of modern times.
But the aimless dispersion characteristic of modern
scientific societies would have been repugnant to
them.   Science to them was not a barren collection
of disconnected truths indiscriminately massed together without reference to their bearing on the
social interests of the human race ; it was the
foundation-stone of a vast edifice destined for the
aggrandizement and ennobling of human life.   In
their very errors there was much that was not only
noble and grand, but profoundly useful.   Descartes'
theory of vortices was a bold scaffolding of con-
jecture thrown out to hold together isolated facts,
till Newton's memorable discovery of the laws of
gravitation, prepared as it was by the previous

efforts of Kepler, Galileo, and Huygens, destroyed it by replacing it.

I do not propose, in this course of Lectures, to give any synopsis, however brief, of the literature of the period. I only touch upon it to illustrate the historical principles upon which we have all along been proceeding. In studying the movement of European thought in the seventeenth century, it is impossible to avoid allusion to the place which Art and Poetry occupy in that movement. The works of Shakespeare, Cervantes, and Molière belong to all future ages. But they belong also, in a peculiar sense, to their own age. Their production was an historical event of great magnitude, the significance of which it is worth while attempting to appreciate.

The periods of history distinguished for great works of art are very few. In the twenty-seven or twenty-eight centuries of which the evolution of Western Europe consists, we shall find not more than seven, speaking roughly, which have produced works destined to be immortal. If we leave out the periods of Homer and Hesiod, of Æschylus and Aristophanes, of Lucretius and Lucan, of Dante and Petrarch, of Ariosto and Tasso, of Shakespeare and Racine, of Goethe and Scott (I have chosen for the most part names that mark the limits of each period), we shall find twenty-one centuries, each of them with its own peculiar importance as a link in the chain of progress, but poetically barren. The Aloetree of Poetry has very seldom blossomed.

Of the laws which regulate this distribution of talent, many lie, no doubt, and will probably for a long time lie, beyond our analysis. It seems clear,

however, that many of the conditions favourable for
poetic growth have very seldom existed, and that all
of them have never as yet existed simultaneously.
Periods of intense activity either in building up or in
pulling down, periods of intense struggle, whether
mental or physical, are not likely to leave vigorous
minds at leisure for verse-making.   The building up
of the Roman Empire, or of the early Christian
Church, the struggle of the Reformation in Northern
Europe, the revolutionary logic of the eighteenth
century, were processes of over-intense and one-sided
vitality ; utterly foreign to that calm, harmonious,
and many - sided development of human powers
which Art requires.   It must be owned, too, though
the discussion of the point would lead me far from
my province, that Art and Religion have seldom or
never lent that mutual assistance of which some
partial fruit was seen in the days of Homer and of
Phidias, and of which far richer results lie no doubt
before us in times to come.   The metaphysical
theology of the Middle Ages was not propitious,
and this Dante knew, either to poetry or painting :
and Raphael's Madonnas, like the Sybils and
Prophets of Michael Angelo, indicate an ideal
Future rather than a venerated Past.

Be this as it may, it would seem that the times
most favourable to the rise of great poets have been
those brief intervals of calm immediately following
or preceding a great crisis.   The excitement of a
political storm, acting on those who stand on its
verge, spectators but not partakers, has been the
stimulus, so history teaches, to great poets.   Athens
in the century after Marathon and Salamis ; Rome

when the civil wars and the work of conquest were over, and the *pax Romana* was established ; Florence of the fourteenth century, triumphant in the long contest with the German Emperors ; Italy in the sixteenth century, stimulated by the Renaissance, and yet saved from the noise and turmoil of the Lutheran outbreak ; England in the interval between the Reformation and the Commonwealth,—enjoyed the calm of which I speak, the calm not of death, but of strong sensitive life.

And such a time was the middle of the seventeenth century for France. The religious wars were over ; the victory over Spain without and the feudal aristocracy within had been fully won ; the national unity had been strongly constituted, the national forces wrought to a high pitch ; everything pointed to an immediate future of vigorous, peaceful, harmonious development. It was not a time of intense activity in pulling down or building up ; or rather the process of demolition, as I have pointed out before, was confined as yet to a small number of minds. The age of Richelieu and of Colbert was singularly favourable to all the peaceful arts of life ; and above all, to that highest of the arts, that production of idealized types of human nature which we call Poetry.

For the Poetry of the Western nations has been from its very outset positive and humanist in its character. Even with Homer, whose polytheistic machinery played so important a part as to have given rise to the superficial notion that he invented the popular mythology, even in the *Iliad* and *Odyssey*, the human interests rise immeasurably superior to

L

the super-human.    Even in Æschylus, even in Dante,
this is the case ; and how much more so in Ariosto,
in Shakespeare, in Corneille !    Indeed, it is not too
much to say that the positive study of human nature,
in which the greatest philosophic intellects have
made hitherto such slender progress, has been cultivated almost exclusively by the great poets of
Western Europe.    Nor is this singular.    The science
of human nature only follows in this respect the
history of other sciences ; all of which have originated, as Geometry originated, in their corresponding
arts, in the practical and empirical pursuits of
common life.    From the pedantry of metaphysicians,
who reduce the study of human nature to its purely
intellectual aspects, or who, if they treat of the moral
side at all, endeavour to reduce all human motives
to self-interest ; from the narrowness of theologians,
who reiterate only that human nature is simply and
totally corrupt,—we take refuge with the poets who
show us Man as he really is ; removing indeed the
mere accidents of his life, the clogs and cumbrous
appendages of destiny and chance, and placing him
in a free, clear medium, where the complex play of
rival sympathies and passions becomes for the first
time visible.    Examine the seven or eight hundred
characters of Shakespeare's dramas ; how many
totally corrupt persons will you find there ?    Hardly
three.    Not even in Milton's Lucifer will you find
total corruption ; and there are germs of unselfish
tenderness in the lowest circles of Dante's Hell.

Every great poet then has, in his own implicit
and empirical way, added fresh materials for the
study of man's moral powers ; has prepared the way

for the highest of all sciences,—the science of Human Nature. And on this ground alone the century of Shakespeare's *Lear* and *Hamlet*, of the *Don Quixote* of Cervantes, of Corneille's *Cid, Horace*, and *Polyeucte*, of Molière's *Tartuffe*, of Racine's *Athalie*, of Calderon's *Magico prodigioso*, and of Milton's *Paradise Lost*, claims immortal praise. Poets have been called philosophers. It would seem unwise to confound two words required for two such different modes of mental activity. But it is true to say that the intellectual powers called into play are very nearly identical in both ; and that great poets, born in another age, would have been great philosophers. The first process of the mind is the same in both. Both begin by Abstraction. Both abstract or clear away from their object many of the properties which in actual life it may possess, concentrating their attention on certain special qualities. There the resemblance between them ends. The philosopher abstracts in order to generalize ; the poet in order to idealize. The philosopher abstracts or selects certain qualities from objects in order to find the general principle or law common to these qualities ; the poet selects certain aspects of man (rejecting others) in order to heighten them, to increase their force, to put them into fuller prominence.

Let it not be forgotten that the poet's mission has its practical side. His office, as Aristotle said long ago, is κάθαρσις τῶν πάθων ; that is to say, by terror, by sympathy, by ridicule, to purify the passions ; not indeed to preach pedantic truisms, or rose-coloured benevolence, for the poet is no moralist or preacher, but to represent the play of conflicting

passions strongly and faithfully, clearing them only
from the low, the common, the paltry, and the
trivial. The poet has no call to turn away from
life's darker side. No crimes were so deadly but
Dante could find a place for them in his *Inferno*;
those alone among the damned of whom he could
say nothing, scathing them as he passes by with
speechless scorn, being those who were neither good
nor bad, neither faithful to God nor to his enemies,
*ma per se furo*, who lived only for themselves.
Choosing from the confused prosaic mass of life its
broader, larger, grander aspects, whether dark or
bright, aggrandizing what is noble, aggrandizing no
less, if need be, what is fierce and hateful, then fusing
the conflicting parts into a perfect whole, dominating
his angry discords by sovereign harmonies, the poet
raises men from the dust, purges their passions of
the petty griefs and joys that have clogged and
choked them, sweeps for a while the dull disguise of
triviality away, and makes us 'feel that we are
greater than we know.'

The place thus occupied by the great poets
(among whom, I need hardly say, are to be included
the great masters of form, colour, and sound), in the
world's history is very high. They are not philosophers; yet they supply in richer abundance than
metaphysicians or theologians the materials for
the scientific Theory of Human Nature. They are
not moral preachers; yet by contagious sympathy
they lift us unconsciously, without will or effort, to a
higher atmosphere, where we have at least the chance,
if we so resolve, to stay. I speak here, of course, of
the very small number of great poets, not of the

mediocre mass, whom neither gods nor men should
tolerate.     And of that small minority were assuredly
Molière and Pierre Corneille.    It is not too much to
say that the nobler features of the French character,
the fearless frankness, the keen sense of honour, the
brilliant sense, above all the unsparing hatred of
cant, which are prominent among French virtues,
have been strengthened and heightened by the
efforts of these two great men.    Molière is known
moderately well, though not well enough, in England, as in every other part of the civilized world ;
Corneille is known to us by name, and very little
more.    The loss is ours, and I venture to say it is a
very serious loss.    One reason is, perhaps, that no
great poet ever produced so many works which,
though grand in parts, yet as a whole are faulty.
But if those who open him for the first time limit
their reading to his four masterpieces, the *Cid*, the
*Horace*, the *Cinna*, and the *Polyeucte*, they will find
themselves brought face to face with a spirit of
heroic stamp.    They had best put all comparisons
with the great English dramatist utterly aside.
Between the 'myriad-minded' magician of our own
land, and the manly, limited, straightforward simpli-
city of Corneille, there is no similarity whatever.
If Corneille is to be compared to other poets, it
should be to the Greek dramatists, to Virgil and
Lucan, or to our own Milton.    The motive in
each of his works is simple and usually the same ;
the conflict between private and public passions,
between love and duty, between love and honour,
between love and religion ; eternal problems which
will vex the noblest natures to the end of time.    It

is not for the artist to solve the problem, to give the victory to either of the combatant passions. His it is simply to array either foe in his strongest armour, to strain the energies of both to the highest, then to portray the conflict, and let the nobler sympathies of those who witness it take their free course.

But detailed criticism of Corneille's poetry must not detain us. We have only to allude to its bearing as an historical event of the seventeenth century. And from this aspect there is one further remark to be made. Corneille entered more systematically than any previous poet into a domain where the great poets of future times may find an exhaustless harvest : the domain of history. To the idealization of the successive phases of Roman history, a field into which Shakespeare, with what glorious success we know, had entered before him, he devotes no less than twelve dramas. In the movement of European thought during the seventeenth century, the culture of the historical sense thus promoted in the most powerful way by Corneille is not to be overlooked. Nor should the *chef-d'œuvre* of Racine, his *Athalie*, less powerful perhaps, but of such consummate perfection in form as no poet north of the Alps has rivalled, be passed by.

Molière too must be noticed from the historical point of view solely. His direct influence on social and mental progress is perhaps greater than that of any other poet. His attacks on all that was most retrograde and most powerful in his time, on theological hypocrisy, on metaphysical pedantry, on aristocratic frivolity, well merit mention in the series of influences of which the French Revolution was the issue. Thoroughly penetrated as he was with the Positive and Republican spirit, dreaded by the clergy, hated by the aristocracy, his existence at the Court of Louis XIV is a singular anomaly. The storm aroused by his writings was such that, but for the King's protection, he could not have lived in it an hour. Molière died before Louis XIV became fatally retrograde. The shelter that Louis gave to Molière is, it has been said, his best title to the gratitude of posterity.

We are now in a position to appreciate more distinctly what was briefly alluded to at the beginning of this lecture,—the religious movement of the seventeenth century. We shall not lose much by confining our review to France, where each extreme phase of the religious world was developed to its height, and where many intermediate phases may be seen which elsewhere are less distinct. In France the philosophic movement was most intense ; equally intense, therefore, was the movement of reaction. The two great rival camps, Protestant and Catholic, which elsewhere were separated, in France were brought into close and intimate contact. In Holland, in Great Britain, in Sweden, the worship of the Mass was, for the greater part of the century, as rigidly prohibited as the Calvinistic sermon in Italy or Spain. Protestantism neither inculcated toleration, nor even professed to inculcate it. For the toleration which we now enjoy we have to thank neither of the rival sects, but rather the statesmen and philosophers who utilized their mutual antagonism so as to procure a compromise. How Richelieu effected this equilibrium of the two religions in Europe has been already shown ; and what the Continent gained by the treaty of Westphalia, France had gained fifty years before by the Edict of Nantes. By that edict the French Protestants, who numbered perhaps a tenth of the total population, 2,000,000 out of 20,000,000, obtained absolute liberty of conscience ; performance of public worship in 3,500 castles, as well as in certain specified towns in each province ; a state endowment equal to £20,000 a year ; civil rights equal in every respect to those of Catholics ; admission to all public colleges, hospitals, &c. ; finally, eligibility to all offices of State. Two hundred towns which they had occupied during the religious wars, chiefly in Poitou, Guienne, Languedoc, and Dauphiné, were to be for several years exclusively occupied by Protestants ; the Governors in all cases to be of their religion.   They secured also the right of holding assemblages where the political as well as the religious interests of their body were decided on.   This right of assembly, vested in a body holding 200 garrisoned towns, constituted an *imperium in imperio*, and was a state of things that could not last.   The public declaration of one of their synods in 1603, that 'the bishop of Rome was properly the antichrist and the son of perdition foretold in the Word of God under the emblem of the whore clothed in scarlet,' and a long series of violent intolerances like those described by Mr. Buckle, indicated no wish to avail themselves wisely and peaceably of their admirable position as the only tolerated minority in Europe.   At last their pretensions rose to the level of rebellion.

Richelieu spent two years of his valuable life in besieging their stronghold. The capture of La Rochelle removed what, for nearly a century, had been one of the great obstacles to the unity of France, one of the most obvious stepping-stones for feudal ambition. Richelieu crushed Protestantism in France so far as it was a separate political organization claiming to exercise separate sovereignty. But he scrupulously protected Protestants in their equal civil rights, as secured to them by the Edict of Nantes.

Mazarin, and after Mazarin, Colbert, followed in the same track. Many of the most important manufactures which Colbert was so anxious to encourage were carried on by Protestants ; and he found amongst them many men fit for important financial posts. Louis XIV, though personally disliking the Protestants, yet in his memoirs, written in 1670, expressly lays down the duty of leaving the Act of Toleration undisturbed. Up to the time when his Government became retrograde, and Colbert's influence sank before that of the Jesuits and of Louvois—up to the time, that is to say, of the war with Holland—the Protestants held a position in France which strangely contrasts with the severity of the legislation against Catholics enacted during the same period in England and Ireland. And yet, with all these advantages, their numbers during the whole of this period, and indeed from the beginning of the century, had been steadily diminishing ; partly from the tendency of the dominant religion in every country to absorb those whose conformity to either sect is merely nominal and outward ; partly also from the inherent logical weakness of the Protestant position.

Let us turn to the opposite camp. We find it united against all outsiders ; by no means united within itself. I have explained already that, in the innumerable attempts that have been made since the close of the Middle Ages to reconstruct out of the ruins of the old Catholic system some imperfect and temporary shelter, each of these partial reformations based itself on some isolated portion of the old doctrine, rejecting the rest. The Protestants were broadly distinguished from the Catholics in rejecting the Church and taking their stand upon the Bible. But there was bitter dissension within the Catholic no less than within the Protestant camp as to the particular direction in which to conciliate, the exact point at which to stand fast.

Of these attempts to reconstruct, that of the Jesuits was by far the boldest, the ablest, and ultimately the most dangerous and noxious. The Catholics from the fourteenth century, and almost every sect of Protestants afterwards, had abandoned the great political principle of the Middle Ages,— the separation and independence of the spiritual power. Long before the Reformation the kings of Europe had placed themselves above the popes. The reformation of Ignatius Loyola aimed at nothing less than the re-establishment of Papal independence. They saw very clearly that a Church subordinate to the State is no Church in the proper sense at all. The dogmas of State churches would become, as they knew, fixed institutions of the country, very difficult to modify without a political convulsion, con-

sequently certain to grow more and more out of har-
mony with the changing spirit of the age.  But a
European church wholly independent of any particular
State, could modify its institutions, and even its doctrines, as need might arise.  And in such modification
the Jesuits were prepared to go great lengths.  They
saw how the scheme of Catholic doctrine had
branched out into full development in the course
of centuries from its germ in the New Testament.
They were prepared, no doubt, for further development in the future.  Certain it is, at least, that they
alone among the Catholic sects dared to face and to
accept the intellectual movement of the age.  No
Protestant sect has approached the wisdom and
largeness of their educational system.  In this
respect at least it must be allowed that their means
have been better than their ends.

Doubtless their aim of re-establishing the spiritual
power was wholly chimerical and hopeless, and by
the abler and more honest of the body it was soon
seen to be so.  I have already pointed out the
distinction that is to be made between the first
generation of Jesuits and their successors.  Towards
the end of the sixteenth century, and during the
whole of the seventeenth century, all that is noblest
amongst them is to be found in foreign missions.
In India, in China, in Paraguay, their fearless and
untiring devotion, and their wise conciliating spirit,
had free scope.  The history of the Chinese mission
alone is sufficient to redeem them from the foolish
sneers of Protestant writers.  Their introduction of
Western science into China, their acceptance of the
two great institutions of the country, the worship of

Heaven and the worship of Ancestors, as a common basis of sympathy on which to work, contrasts strangely with the narrower spirit of Protestant missionaries. It was indeed, as might be imagined, far too liberal for the rest of the Catholic world, and the discussions that took place in Europe upon 'Chinese ceremonies' is not the least important feature in the religious history of the seventeenth century.

As much cannot be said of the Jesuits in Europe. To the last, indeed, they remained distinguished from the other Catholic sects for practical wisdom, knowledge of the world, and successful education of the young. But the pursuit of their political ideal, chimerical at the best, degenerated at last, when followed by men of narrower minds and lower characters, into unscrupulous intrigue. Their simultaneous suppression by every Catholic Government in the eighteenth century, marked the avowed impotence of the old religion to avail itself of the only philosophical attempt to adapt it to modern progress.

Opposed to the Jesuits stood the Jansenists. A phase of faith which attracted the great intellect of Pascal, and grouped together such men as Saint-Cyran, Arnauld, Nicole, and the poet Racine, cannot be passed over in silence. The general history of Port-Royal is more familiar to Protestant even than to Catholic readers. The Port-Royalists were the Calvinists of Catholicism. Their attempt at reconstruction embraced exactly those parts of the mediæval religion which the Jesuits had neglected. Wholly abandoning what the Jesuits had taken hold of, the social and political side of Catholicism, they clung to its personal, mystical, and ascetic side. Like the Protestants, they reverenced St. Augustine beyond all other divines. They drew out into prominence doctrines which the wiser instinct of the mediæval theologians had usually left in the background. The damnation of unbaptized infants, the necessity of prevenient grace, and its corollary doctrine, the predestination of every human soul before its birth to salvation or damnation, were points on which their authors loved to dwell. With them, as with the Calvinists, such doctrines formed the basis of stern ascetic discipline, by which they vainly hoped to resist and remedy the general corruption of society around them. The doctrine of election, clearly stated by Augustine, and revived by Calvin and Jansen, had been always kept in the background by the Catholic hierarchy. They feared its tendency to subvert all spiritual discipline and subordination by elevating the humblest and most ignorant to an equal or a higher level than their superiors. There was latent revolution in the doctrine ; and indeed in Scotland, Holland, and Geneva it had been anything but latent. It was singular, too, that many of the leaders in the insurrection of the Fronde had been Jansenists. For these things they became suspicious in the eyes of the authorities in Church and State. Moreover, the severity and inflexibility of their moral code was especially repugnant to the Jesuits. The Jesuits were saving society, or attempting to save it, by making themselves all things to all men ; modifying their moral standard to suit men of the world ; pushing conciliation to its extreme length, and

indeed often far beyond it. Jansenism they thought
dangerous, because by its severity it drove men out
of the pale of the Church altogether. For all these
reasons Jansenism became suspicious in the eyes of
the authorities in Church and State. The Jesuits,
their temper by no means sweetened by Pascal's
*Provincial Letters,* attacked them under ground and
above ground, at Court, and at the Vatican, in the
pulpit, and in the *salons* of Paris. The Pope fulminated several fierce Bulls against them. Louis XIV
in his memoirs warns his son to discourage them
in every possible way.[1] It seems that Louis XIV
in his old age was not quite alive to the signs of
the times. Few of the spiritual guides of France
seem to have been less blind. Certain it is that
during the last years of Louis XIV Catholicism was
being torn to shreds by the dissensions of its own
children. The Bull *Unigenitus* was the best possible
preparation for the *Encyclopédie.*

One man there was, and one only, in the Catholic
world, who strove in a large and philosophic spirit to
meet the danger. Bossuet, bishop of Meaux, a man
of character and intellect worthy of the best days of
the Mediæval Church, stood forward to defend her,

[1] St. Simon tells us that the Duke of Orleans, the King's nephew,
afterwards Regent, on the occasion of a journey to Spain, requested
that a certain Montpertuis should be allowed to join his suite : 'A
ce nom voilà le roi qui prend un air austère ; Comment, mon neveu,
Montpertuis, le fils de cette janséniste, de cette folle qui a couru M.
Arnaud partout ! Je ne veux point de cet homme-là avec vous !
Ma foi, Sire, je ne sais pas ce qu'a fait la mère, mais pour le fils,
il n'a garde d'être janséniste, et je vous en réponds ; car il ne croit
pas en Dieu ! Est-il possible, mon neveu ? répliqua le roi, en se
radoucissant. Rien de plus certain, Sire. Puisque cela est, il
n'y a point de mal : vous pouvez le mener.'—Quoted by Martin,
*Hist. de France,* vol. xiv, p. 602.

if that were possible, from foes without and from the
still more threatening peril of decay within.  Had
Troy been to be saved, his would have been the right
arm to save it.   He saw the true grandeur of the
Catholic structure, even in its ruin ; venerable even
to sceptics, and against Protestants impregnable.   His
*History of the Variations of the Protestant Churches*,
in which, quoting Luther, Melanchthon, Zwingli, and
Calvin, with as few words as possible of his own, he
allows each to overthrow the other ; and shows how
much self-contradiction is inherent in the nature of a
theory which, while clinging to divine revelation,
rejects the divine authority of the Church, must be
looked upon, even by those who reject its conclusion,
as a masterpiece of vigorous and temperate controversy.   His short tract, entitled *Exposition of the
Catholic Faith*, made more converts among the French
Protestants than Louvois's dragonnades.   The great
Protestant general Turenne was among the first to be
convinced by it.   As a simple, clear, and philosophic
statement of the Catholic dogma, cleared from all its
non-essential accessories, it is well worth reading,
either by those who wish to judge their opponents
candidly, or by all thoughtful students of the history
of the human mind.   His works present a complete
view of Catholicism as a coherent synthesis, intellectual, social, and political.   His *Politique tirée de
l'Écriture Sainte*, or System of Polity based upon the
language of Holy Scripture, is precisely what its
title indicates : a Philosophy of Government from
the theocratic point of view.   As a consistent and
logical development of the theory of Divine Right of
Kings, this treatise is of permanent historical value.

Its contemporary value in stimulating political
thought in precisely the opposite direction, was no
doubt very great.    A great debt is due to the man
who brings out a system of belief, whether true or
false, into full daylight.    Mystification is a far worse
danger than error.    'Give us light,' said Ajax, 'even
if we die for it.'    Bossuet's *Politique Sacrée* led by
natural revulsion to Rousseau's *Contrat social ;* the
divine Right of kings, to the abstract Rights of
Man.    The long struggle between these two theories,
neither of them superior in rationality to the other,
clears the way for a final theory of human relations,
founded neither on supernatural dogma nor on metaphysical abstractions, but on the scientific study of
the historical Evolution of Humanity.

Bossuet's theory of government did not include
the principle of Toleration, any more than did that
of his great Protestant opponent, Jurieu.    Both distinctly lay it down as the duty of Government to
discourage and suppress religious error by persuasion
if possible, but if necessary by force.    Toleration like
that sanctioned by the edict of Nantes was wholly
inconsistent with any theory of government then
existing.    The great English philosopher, Hobbes,
held distinctly that a State religion, which it should
be criminal to attack, was, as a mere measure of
police, most desirable.    The severity of the penal
laws against Dissenters and Catholics in England
and Ireland, so far from diminishing, had steadily
increased since the Restoration.    The revocation of
the Edict of Nantes, therefore, foolish and disastrous
as it was, and as it was thought to be by Colbert
and by all who had the commercial prosperity of

the country at heart, was in strict accordance with the principles then prevailing in Protestant as well as Catholic countries.   But though Bossuet cordially accepted the edict of Revocation, it is certain that had his voice been listened to, France would have been spared the disgrace of the brutal persecutions which followed it ; the most disgraceful persecutions, because the most needless and gratuitous, in the whole history of religious intolerance.   There was no danger of France becoming Protestant ;   the whole antecedents of the country, the logical and yet sympathetic character of the people, had evidently decided that question a century ago.   France, remaining nominally Catholic, was preparing for far deeper changes than any that Luther or Calvin had ever dreamt of.   There was not the slightest tendency, nor had there ever been since the conversion of Henry of Navarre, to an increase in the Protestant numbers.   The Catholic faith had provisionally been adopted by almost all thinking men.   Rejected by almost every important intellect in France, Protestantism might safely have been left to its natural process of decay.   The Dragonnades, and the persecution of the Port-Royalists, illustrate that deep saying of the Middle Ages, that madness comes first on those who are destined for destruction.   They aroused strange rebellious thoughts in young minds whose lips were not yet loosed.

The last years of Louis XIV's reign are dull and dreary, and merit no remembrance.   Most of the great generals, statesmen, and poets of the age of Richelieu and Colbert had passed away.   The

M

intellectual stagnation of France has indeed been
considerably exaggerated by recent writers.[1]    But
it is certain that intellectual life was at a low ebb in
France.   One fact is sufficient to prove it.   Newton's discovery of the law of Gravitation remained
unaccepted, and indeed almost unknown in France,
for a generation after it had been circulated in
England.   Yet as we tread the weary desert of
those years of physical misery, dead formality,
spiritual tyranny, and political disgrace, we scent
from afar the fresh breeze of Ocean, we hear its
distant roar.   The greatest Revolution in the world's
history was nigh at hand, and France, Jesuit-ridden
and paralysed as she might seem, was destined to
give it birth.   At the death of Louis XIV, D'Alembert was not yet born ; Diderot and Rousseau were
in their cradles.   But Montesquieu was approaching
manhood ; and there was another young spirit who
for some years had been watching the world around
him with eager and impatient scorn, waiting like a
wild beast chained, till the cry of joy that rang
through France at the King's death should give the
signal for the combat.   His name was François
Marie Arouet, commonly called Voltaire.

## NOTE TO LECTURE IV

Michelet remarks, with some truth, that the
age of Louis XIV ended everything and initiated
nothing.   It is certain that the greatest names of
the seventeenth century belong rather to the period

[1] See Note appended to this Lecture.

of Richelieu or of Mazarin than to that of Louis XIV. Mr. Buckle, so far as I know, is the first English writer who has brought this fact into full prominence. But it must be said also that he exaggerates it. 'Louis XIV,' he says, 'survived the entire intellect of the French nation, except that small part of it which grew up in opposition to his principles. . . . Several years before his death, . . . there was no popular liberty, there were no great men, there was no science, there was no literature ; there were no arts.' 'If we examine the fifty-four years of his reign, from 1661 to 1715, we shall be struck by the remarkable fact, that everything which is celebrated was effected in the first half of it.'[1]   I will not lay stress on the fact that Racine's *chef-d'œuvre* was published in the latter half of the period.   But we must not forget that this period could still boast of such theologians as Bossuet, Fénelon, and Bourdaloue ; of the Church historian Fleury ; of such philosophers as Malebranche, Bayle, and Fontenelle ; of such mathematicians as L'Hôpital and Varignon ; of the great botanist Tournefort ; of Sauveur the founder of acoustics ; of Lahire the astronomer ; of the two Delisles, the geographers.   Fénelon and Malebranche died in the same year as Louis XIV ; Varignon, the Delisles, Lahire, Sauveur, Fleury, and Fontenelle survived him ; to say nothing of Voltaire and Montesquieu, the first of whom was twenty-one years of age at Louis's death, the latter twenty-six.   These names are certainly not all of them among the greatest ; nor would I dispute Mr. Buckle's main position, that the patronage of Louis was less

[1] Buckle, *History of Civilization*, vol. i, pp. 649, 653.

favourable to intellectual development than has been represented ; but they show that at least Louis did not 'survive the entire intellect of France,' that the intellectual filiation of France was not wholly broken off. It is singular that writers who are the most eager to maintain that governments are powerless for good, are the most prone to exaggerate not merely their wish to do mischief, but their power to do it.

THE END

*Printed by* R. & R. CLARK, LIMITED, *Edinburgh*.

## BY THE SAME AUTHOR

A GENERAL VIEW OF POSITIVISM. Translated from the French of Auguste Comte. With an Introduction by FREDERIC HARRISON. 1s. net. (George Routledge and Sons.)

THE UNITY OF COMTE'S LIFE AND DOCTRINE. An Answer to J. S. MILL. 1s. net. (Watts and Co.)

ILLUSTRATIONS OF POSITIVISM. A Selection of Articles from the *Positivist Review*. Edited by E. S. BEESLY. 1s. 6d. net. (Watts and Co.)

ESSAYS AND ADDRESSES. With an Introduction by FREDERIC HARRISON. 8vo. 12s. 6d. net. (Chapman and Hall.)

THE "OPUS MAJUS" OF ROGER BACON. With Introduction and Analytical Table. Three vols. 8vo. 31s. 6d. (Williams and Norgate.)

# WORKS BY
# JOHN RICHARD GREEN

A SHORT HISTORY OF THE ENGLISH PEOPLE. Crown 8vo. 8s. 6d.

A SHORT HISTORY OF THE ENGLISH PEOPLE. Illustrated Edition. Edited by Mrs. J. R. GREEN and Miss KATE NORGATE. With Fourteen hundred Illustrations. Four volumes. Super Royal 8vo. 10s. net each.

THE HISTORY OF THE ENGLISH PEOPLE. In Eight vols. Globe 8vo. 4s. net each.

THE MAKING OF ENGLAND. In Two vols. Globe 8vo. 8s. net.

THE CONQUEST OF ENGLAND. In Two vols. Globe 8vo. 8s. net.

STRAY STUDIES FROM ENGLAND AND ITALY. Globe 8vo. 4s. net.

STRAY STUDIES. Second Series. Globe 8vo. 4s. net.

OXFORD STUDIES. Globe 8vo. 4s. net.

HISTORICAL STUDIES. Globe 8vo. 4s. net.

THE LETTERS OF J. R. GREEN. Edited by Sir LESLIE STEPHEN. 8vo. 15s. net.

MACMILLAN AND CO., LTD., LONDON.